MW01169004

Praise for

DROP ME AROUND THE CORNER

"After devouring the first chapter of Tracy Bouvier's *Drop Me Around the Corner*, I was hooked. I felt like I was right there. I couldn't wait to enjoy the rest of the book. Very engaging."

> —ROGER FISHER, lead guitarist for the rock and
> roll band Heart

"Tracy Bouvier has mined not gold but brass in this volume about growing up with her father, a man who became a legend by driving a van completely covered in brass items around the streets of Burbank, CA. (People still talk about him today!) You can almost feel her teenage embarrassment as he drove her to school, but love conquers all, and this book works as a fond reminiscence of an innocent time and a definitely unique father. A memoir you will ponder once you finish it—can somebody please option this out for a teleplay? You will not be disappointed by this gal's story!"

> —WES CLARK, coauthor of *Lost Burbank, Growing Up
> in Burbank* and *True Tales from Burbank*

"Tracy's prose moves at the pace of memory, making her unique coming-of-age into a satisfying story of off-beat love and lives well lived that you won't soon forget."

> —DAVID FARRIS, award-winning author of *Lie Still*

"Tracy Bouvier's memorable coming-of-age story candidly reveals what it's like to grow up the child of a very charismatic and eccentric father—Ernie Steingold. I found it especially fascinating to read about Tracy's reaction to such a paradoxical single parent. A simple vacuum repairman by trade, Ernie was a man who, outside of work, derived such pleasure and vanity from his muscular body and his outlandish California fantasy van. I found myself smiling a lot as I turned the pages of this unusual and honest memoir."

—**HARROD BLANK**, independent filmmaker, author of
Art Cars, the Artists, the Obsession, the Craft

"Raising a father is hard work, and in *Drop Me Around the Corner*, Tracy Steingold Bouvier celebrates the child inside the man in this endearing memoir about two generations growing up together."

—**ERIN HOSIER**, *Tell Me About Your Father* podcast,
and author of *Don't Let Me Down*

"*Drop Me Around the Corner* is a rollicking tale of Tracy Bouvier's free-range childhood in sunny Burbank, CA, during the 1970s. It is a compelling story of a family finding its way after the devastating loss of a beloved wife and mother. For Tracy and her siblings, life changed dramatically as her father's behavior became more eccentric and flamboyant. Her father was loving but by any measure somewhat inattentive. Tracy does a masterful job of describing her teen angst with heartbreaking, hilarious, and horrifying tales of her extraordinary and often bizarre upbringing."

—**MARIA HECKINGER**, author *of Beyond the Third Door*

"*Drop Me Around the Corner* is hilarious, heartbreaking, and, yes, even a little embarrassing. I laughed. I cheered. I wept. (Plus I would LOVE a ride in that van!)"

—**CAROL LYNCH WILLIAMS**, author of the
award-winning novel *The Chosen One*

DROP ME AROUND
THE CORNER

Drop Me Around the Corner
by Tracy Bouvier

© Copyright 2024 Tracy Bouvier

ISBN 979-8-88824-496-8

Published by

 köehlerbooks™

3705 Shore Drive
Virginia Beach, VA 23455
800-435-4811
www.koehlerbooks.com

DROP ME AROUND THE CORNER

A Memoir

TRACY BOUVIER

VIRGINIA BEACH
CAPE CHARLES

With love to Allison and Steve,
and in loving memory of my mom and dad,
and my nephew Hayden Steingold

TABLE OF CONTENTS

AUTHOR'S NOTE

Events described in this book and stories about my family are written from my perspective. I remember many of the events in great detail. Still, my brother and sister and some of my friends might tell it differently or they might not even remember or know some of it at all. With that being said, the stories in this book are true. The names in the book I've kept true, for the most part.

0
Daddy, Please!

On a hot autumn afternoon in 1964, a naked baby crawled around the pool deck of her family home in Burbank, California. Her father was in a lounge chair wearing one of his trademark bikinis, catching a tan like he often did when the weather was right, which it usually was in The Golden State. He could hear his baby cooing and the birds singing in the trees.

Ernie Steingold wasn't particularly tired that day, but perhaps the sun put him in a trance. Even when he heard a splash and the cooing stop, he didn't move.

Seconds ticked by.

It didn't faze him. He kept on laying there, feeling the sun soak into his bones.

More seconds passed.

Then, it registered. *She's in the pool!*

Ernie gasped and rushed to look in the water. The baby was hovering near the bottom, face down, her arms and legs sprawled out like a soaring eagle, as if she was peacefully enjoying the moment.

Her father hurried down the steps, scooped her up, and she giggled in his arms. He could breathe again. He looked around to see if a neighbor had noticed. Then, as if nothing happened, he put his baby back on the deck, adjusted his lounger, and continued basking in the sun.

He was a bodybuilder with large pectoral muscles and well-defined abs. His bald head was bronzed and shiny and his sideburns were large and dark. Ernie had worked on his body and his tan ever since he was a teenager. His physique and appearance were very important to him. He also worked hard to make a living, enjoyed spending free time with his family, doting over his loving wife, and watching his three kids grow up.

The whole family had been there earlier until his wife took the older ones shopping for shoes, leaving him to watch the baby. This was a strategic move. School was starting Monday, and his wife preferred shopping without a fussy baby in tow.

The temperature was perfect. No need to go into the water. The Santa Ana winds were calm, making it an ideal day to enhance a tan. He looked at the baby from time to time. She was gazing into the water, mesmerized by her own reflection. He relaxed and closed his eyes.

Five minutes later, he heard another splash. He popped up and scooped her out of the water before she sank to the bottom. Yet again, she was giggling.

This was my dad, my neglector and savior, which became a pattern for the rest of my life.

Later, when my mother returned, Dad didn't breathe a word about me being at the bottom of the pool. That day would become our secret, which he didn't tell me about until several years later.

"Your mother would have never forgiven me."

I loved it when he told me that. It reminded me of how much she loved me. I wonder though, would Dad have been different if Mom hadn't died when I was seven? My brother, sister, and I were free to do most anything we wanted.

Life was pure chaos. That's just how Ernie Steingold rolled.

1

California Dreamin'

According to Dad, I wasn't planned, and Mom didn't want to breastfeed me. Be that as it may, I was conceived in Detroit, Michigan in 1963, possibly to the Motown sounds of The Marvelettes, Mary Wells, or The Supremes, singing songs like "What Love Has Joined Together," "Standing at the Crossroads of Love," and "We're Only Young Once" by Bunny Paul.

My dad, the oldest of four kids, grew up in the Detroit suburb of Brightmoor, and were the only Jews in their school. Being Jewish was never an issue in Dad's neighborhood, and he seldom felt any discrimination. Once in a while, an ignorant classmate would call him "Jew" or "The Jew," like it was funny or even endearing, but Dad brushed off those benign encounters.

"Those kids didn't know anything from Adam."

Dad's family blended in like any other white Americans, except for the name, Steingold, and their noses, which were profoundly large. To my dismay, we all seemed to have them, and they never got any smaller.

My dad's parents owned a variety store three blocks from their house. "Joe Saves You Dough" was their tagline. My grandfather gave out candy to the neighborhood kids and built a reputation for being generous, quite the opposite from the stereotype of Jews being cheap.

My grandparents sold anything from Levis to small appliances, and Jewish goods, such as halva and kosher sausage. When my dad was old enough, he worked for his parents as a salesman and repair man. He was enthralled with studying manuals and blueprints and could fix all sorts of appliances and vacuums. This skill would rub off on me; I still love fixing things.

I never knew my grandparents. They died when I was young. Grandma Yetta had immigrated as a child from Kiev, and Grandpa Joe was from Russia. Dad once showed me his yarmulke and Hebrew Bible, which he had kept, even though his family wasn't religious. They celebrated Hanukkah and Dad had a bar mitzvah in 1941 when he was thirteen, but that was it.

"We rarely stepped foot in a synagogue. We were too busy working."

My mother was born the same year as my dad and grew up nearby in Marygrove. She never considered going to college and became an incredibly good typist. Her family owned a gas station, and she and her younger siblings helped them run it. In her free time, she liked to dress up and go dancing with her friends and spend weekends sunbathing at the lake. She was known as a sweetheart and a hard worker, the embodiment of a young, beautiful woman thriving in middle-class, Midwestern America—destined to marry young and happily raise a family.

In my mind, my parents were the perfect love story, equipped to conquer the world. They met at the Gray Stone Ballroom in Detroit in 1952. Donna was wearing a glowing white dress that showed off her slender long legs and dark tan. Ernie was smitten the second he laid eyes on her. He thought Mom was the most beautiful woman he had ever seen. Her bright blue eyes (one of the few things from her I inherited) and kind spirit blew him away. She was his idea of a perfect woman, and his heart melted forever.

"Your Mom couldn't resist me either."

She liked his zeal and sense of adventure and was attracted to his strong physique and brilliant smile.

"I rode a big Harley Davidson. That really turned your mom on. She loved my Harley."

Dad was a big fan of Glen Miller and the drumbeats of Benny Goodman.

"It was hard to keep me and your mom off the tabletops."

I don't remember her well, but I like to think of my mom through that vision in my dad's eyes with them dancing together.

Four years before they met, Dad had been honorably discharged from the US Army, where he was a paratrooper and a medic in the Airborne Division. He was never in direct combat since he joined out of high school at the end of WWII, but he made dozens of jumps, provided first aid to his platoon, and received the Victory Medal.

Jumping out of airplanes totally fit his personality. Ever since he was a kid, Ernie Steingold was a daredevil, always jumping over things. As a young man, he hurdled cars and massive street puddles. He showed off to his friends that he was a trained parachutist by leaping out of second story windows and landing perfectly like a pro.

The first thing he did with his Army wages was to buy a 1200cc Harley Davidson with a windshield, leather side bags, and chrome trim galore. He also started his own vacuum cleaner business. Dad was a great salesman and could fix just about anything with a small motor. But riding his Hog was his favorite pastime.

My parents were regulars at the Highwaymen Motorcycle Club, headquartered in Detroit, and they rode their Harleys all over the region. My mom wore her Levis jeans with big cuffs, paired with a leather jacket, just like everyone else in the bike club.

One time, Dad crashed with Mom on the back. A few years after I heard about it, I had my own mishap on a motorcycle. Two actually, and both of them affected me for the rest of my life.

On a warm, spring day, Donna and Ernie took off on a trip around Lake Erie. They were on a country road in Canada when they came around a sharp bend and hit loose gravel. Dad started to lose control and thought he was going to crash into a large pickup truck. Somehow, he was able to lay the bike down and slide to a stop. Mom and Dad didn't go entirely unscathed. The crash shattered the Harley's windshield and Mom got road rash up the side of her leg. As Dad tended to her wounds, an elderly woman came out of a farmhouse, and Dad thought she was coming to help. He was stunned when she handed him a broom and dustpan and ordered him to clean up the mess. After bandaging up Mom's leg, Dad swept up the glass and they rode off into the sunset.

Mom's family was Lutheran, but they weren't religious. When Mom and Dad started dating, her parents couldn't have cared less that he was a Jew. They thought their daughter could do better than a vacuum man, but Ernie was a good guy and treated my mom like a princess. They couldn't ask for anything more.

On a warm summer night, Dad proposed to Mom on the front porch of her parents' house. To celebrate, he brought a bottle of champagne. They drank the entire bottle and became so drunk that Dad didn't feel he could ride his motorcycle home. Neither one of them were ever big drinkers. He ended up sleeping on the couch, and when Mom's parents found him there in the morning they were infuriated. Her parents thought it was highly improper for their daughter's boyfriend to stay overnight no matter where he was sleeping. But when they found out they were engaged, everyone was happy again. My dad had won them over, like he did with just about everyone else.

When Dad went to see his mother that morning to tell her the news, Grandma Yetta went ballistic. She had always pictured her children marrying into Jewish families the way she and her brothers and sisters had done. She never took religion too seriously, but deep in her heart she always wanted to be part of a Jewish community. When she was a child in Russia, it had always been a comfort to her. Although there were synagogues less than a half hour away in the heart of Detroit city, she never connected much with other Jews. Throughout her life, she would always be a Jew living among the gentiles.

"You can't marry a *Shiksa*!"

Grandma Yetta shrieked and fell back on the couch, holding the back of her hand to her forehead.

"I'm going to kill myself."

Dad decided to play along with his melodramatic mother. He walked into the kitchen, grabbed two large knives, and held them up for her to see.

"Which one do you want to use?"

To make life easier for everyone, Mom converted to Judaism. It was easy. All she needed to do was a two-week course in Jewish theology and customs, followed by a meeting with the rabbi. Then she was given a certified document confirming her conversion. As far as Mom was concerned, she was a full-fledged Jew.

My parents married in July 1953. It took a while before they had children. The first was a boy who died in my mom's womb after five months. My poor mother had to go to the hospital to deliver her dead, still baby. The ordeal was so traumatic they put off having more children; three years later my brother, Steve, was born. Looking at photos of him years later, my sister and I would agree that Steve was the ugliest baby we'd ever seen.

Dad had been obsessed with photography since he was a young man. He had a photo lab in the basement of his parent's house, and he took thousands of photos and developed them. Many were of his newborn son. Steve had a big nose and big ears, even as a baby, and for weeks his face had the smashed appearance of a chimpanzee or some kind of mutated Buddha. We couldn't believe that this baby boy was related to us.

Two years later, my sister was born. Without a doubt, Allison was the beautiful doll of the family. She had short, fuzzy blond hair, dark eyes that stared soft and longingly into the camera, and a nose smaller than the rest of us. When we were growing up, I thought Allison was the lucky one. I used to envy her for the great relationship she had with our mother. In home movies and photos, she was always at Mom's side.

I came third in the family lineup, four-and-a-half years after Allison was born. Whether my parents planned for me or not, I arrived

December 18, at Saint Joseph's Hospital in Burbank, California, right next to Walt Disney Studios and just a short ride from Hollywood.

I was a bottle baby, unlike my brother and sister, which may explain a few things, even though I never understood the point of Dad telling me. Why didn't Mom want to breastfeed me? Was he telling me I was a mistake? That her love for me wasn't as strong? Was Dad trying to be funny and thought this would be a good joke? He always thought he was funny. Sometimes he was, but I didn't like his drift on this one.

I have only a scant memory of my mother. All my life I have longed for her love, even now, after I've become a mother myself. Her leaving me so young left me suffering with abandonment issues, and my experiences growing up only compounded that feeling.

We had a drawer in the dining room cabinet filled with family photos. There were countless ones of my mom holding me. She almost always looked so happy. Whether Dad was joking with me or not, she must have loved me. Ironically, I turned out to be a daddy's girl. I wanted to be like him more than anyone.

Still, my parents were adventurers and set their sights on raising a family in California. By 1963, most of my aunts and uncles had moved there, too. It seemed like my whole family were California dreamers. I saw it as their version of the promised land. Eventually, I found my own.

2

All in the Family

Life was close to perfect on Wyoming Avenue. My parents' new house was one-level, Spanish-style, made of stucco with a red terra cotta roof. It had three bedrooms, one bathroom, and the notorious swimming pool.

Mom joined the PTA and made friends with Sandy, a neighbor with two young children close to my age. Dad started a vacuum cleaner business with his brother. Since location was key to being successful, they leased a place in "Beautiful Downtown Burbank," as Johnny Carson used to say on *The Tonight Show*. Uncle Willy manned the store while Dad did repairs in our garage and delivered vacuums to customers across the San Fernando Valley. Mom did the accounting and drummed up business by phone. She was great at convincing people they needed their vacuum serviced and turned out to be quite a salesperson.

Business was booming. Mom loved the money they made and enjoyed the people she met. But after a while, she began to run a little ragged. She was a hands-on parent who attended every PTA meeting, sewed most of the clothes we wore, took care of the household chores and always cooked dinner. Her days were packed. I was there with her all the time, storming around the house, demanding her attention.

When I was three-and-a-half, Dad got home from work one day and found Mom really upset because of me. I had taken off my clothes and escaped down the street, roaming the neighborhood naked. Before

Mom realized what happened, two police officers knocked at the front door. Mom was horrified, as I was wrapped in a survival blanket. She felt like the most neglectful mother in the world.

"Think of what could have happened to her, Ernie."

If a neighbor hadn't recognized me and told the police where I lived, I could have gotten lost, or God knows what.

Dad wasn't as concerned as Mom. Apparently, I had run away naked before and had always come back safe and sound. He thought it was a habit I would outgrow, and I guess it should come as no surprise since Dad often walked around the house naked. We were used to it. I guess it was me trying to be like him, which became a theme for many years to come—Dad downplaying my troubles and mishaps.

Mom could hardly wait until I was in school, so when it came time to sign me up for kindergarten at the end of the summer of 1968, she was livid when she discovered I was seventeen days short of being eligible.

"I can't wait another year!"

When she examined my birth certificate, Mom discovered the font was identical to the one on her typewriter, which made it easy to change the date of my birth. Feeling a strong desire to emancipate herself from a child terrorist, she slipped my birth certificate in the roller of her LC Smith typewriter, placed correction paper over it, and stamped the number 8 key in just the right spot. Like magic, I was now seventeen days older and eligible for kindergarten. The school secretary never looked twice. If she had held the certificate to the light, she would have seen the forgery through the paper.

I ended up the youngest pupil graduating in the class of 1981. Some kids were a full year older than me. Mom and Dad didn't worry about how that affected me. I didn't know at the time just how desperate Mom was to get rid of me so she could have more time to work. Learning this later gave me some of the weird notions of abandonment and doubts about her love for me. I might sound like a poor little whiner, but this stuff matters to a kid.

Meanwhile, Burbank was a perfect suburban town for raising kids. There were great schools, and mine was just around the corner. We lived in the center of town, with safe sidewalks and plush homes divided with cinder block walls that turned our neighborhood into the ultimate playground, where we could walk atop the walls to explore all the backyards. We rode our bikes everywhere and pool hopped at unknowing neighbors just because it was fun.

The foothills of Burbank led to the Angeles Crest Forest. There was the Pickwick horse stables, where you could ride horses around town or into Griffith Park. My parents loved living in the media mecca of the world. Like Hollywood, just over the hill, Burbank was a company town for NBC, Disney, and Warner Brothers, where scenes from your favorite TV shows and hit movies were filmed. It was common to see celebrities at the grocery store or walking their dog. One day, I saw Angie Dickinson doing a car stunt at the corner of Burbank Boulevard and Hollywood Way for her hit show, *Police Woman*. It was exciting, and part of the tapestry of growing up in Burbank.

The best thing about living on Wyoming Avenue was having a pool in our backyard. Everybody loved it. My aunts, uncles and cousins were always lounging around, basking in the sun, drinking beverages, watching us kids swim and dive and giggle. Dad and Uncle Earl liked to launch us into the air and watch us fly into the deep end. The California dream was really working out.

The vacuum business did well because Dad was a wizard at fixing them and women living in the hills of Studio City loved their repairman picking up and dropping off their machines. Sometimes, Dad took me with him on his deliveries in his blue Ford panel van, which I loved. He had a whole routine for sprucing up the vacuums. First, repair and service, then cleaning and polishing, and sometimes he spray painted them. He said if he sent them back looking better than before, they were more likely to become repeat customers. I thought he just liked painting things to make them look cool. That reasoning made perfect sense. Dad had artistic inclinations.

He used to listen to Otis Redding as he worked in the detached garage at the end of our driveway. We could always tell when Dad was painting, not just from the sound of him shaking paint cans, but from the smell of the metallic paint, which was everywhere.

The vacuums were lined up and masked with tape so paint wouldn't get on the Hoover emblem or the rubber bumper around the base. He taught me how far to hold the aerosol nozzle from the vacuum and how to spray in a slow, swaying motion. Then he'd tell me to shake the can again because the metallic paint needed constant stirring. He had a whole assortment of colors. Sometimes he'd sprinkle glitter on them to give it a special touch.

I wondered if his customers knew he was going to paint their vacuums. What if they didn't like the glitter? It seemed risky, but it was Dad's way and I never heard about any complaints.

Spray painting with Dad was fun. Once he made the final touches, we stood back to admire them. He used to say he was the best vacuum man in town. I believed that more than anything, and today, if I smell the scent of spray paint, I am teleported to Dad's garage and the image of all those pretty colorful vacuums.

3

Mom

I can't remember my mother much at all—her voice, the scent of her skin or any opinions she had, but I can picture little things and events that made an impression, like her punching keys on an adding machine in the kitchen with a pencil behind her ear. She seemed so businesslike and attentive. I remember her getting frustrated with me when I burned the pudding because I didn't stir to the bottom like she had told me. Mom used to eat Cream of Rice all the time, too.

The only reason I know it was not Cream of Wheat, the one that was on TV commercials all the time, is because Mom had celiac sprue. If she ate anything with gluten she would get incredibly sick. Other than that, Donna was a healthy, normal young woman—until I turned five.

That's when something in my poor mother's body changed and she became perpetually ill. Most things she ate made her feel sick, and everyone could tell she was never well. She became thinner and her skin turned increasingly yellow. Finally, when I was seven, she was admitted to the hospital, critically malnourished. I didn't see her for days on end. The hospital frowned on lots of visitors, especially young children, so I usually wasn't allowed to see her. They made me sit in the hallway while my two older siblings moved freely in and out of her room. I hated being left out in the hallway on an armless

13

sofa, swinging my legs, pouting, watching people get on and off the elevator. I was bored and longed to see my mom.

Dad continued working and we kept up with our schoolwork the best we could. Eventually, Dad decided to hire a housekeeper to clean and cook some meals because everything seemed to be falling apart.

One day, a hospital administrator pulled Dad aside. The bill was growing, and we had no medical insurance, so he suggested transferring my mother to UCLA Medical Center. In essence, they were kicking Mom out of their hospital over money. I remember hating St Joseph's after that. Every time I drove by there, I got a sour taste in my mouth.

By the time Mom got to UCLA, her liver had gotten so bad she needed to go into the intensive care unit. Soon after, a surgeon called Dad to say that they were taking Mom into emergency surgery for a perforated bowel. Dad, seemingly in denial, continued to work on a vacuum, then stopped at the corner store for a Coke because he got thirsty. According to him, once he started driving home, the words finally hit him. *"Perforated bowel."* That's the moment he suddenly realized how bad that news really was. As he headed down Burbank Boulevard, intense pains radiated through his chest and wouldn't let up, forcing him to pull over. He was short of breath and had broken out into a sweat. It took a few minutes before he felt well enough to drive, and instead of going home he headed straight to the hospital. Many years later, it was determined that Dad probably had a minor heart attack that day, an ailment that would affect him more than we ever knew.

By the time Dad got to the hospital, Mom was out of surgery and in a coma. I had heard the word *coma* a lot back then and became afraid of it. I heard Dad talking to my aunts and uncles on the phone about how sick Mom was, and it sounded like this coma could mean the end of her. I knew it was bad because they wouldn't let me see her in the hospital at all. Back then, no children were allowed in the ICU, not even my older sibs.

But if Mom was going to die, I reasoned, wouldn't they at least let me see her? They wouldn't deny a kid seeing her mother for the last time. I convinced myself that it wasn't that bad. But when the phone calls kept coming and the word coma persisted, I got scared. Allison, too. On those last few nights, we slept with Dad in their California King bed, which made us feel better.

Then the phone rang one night around three. Dad turned on the light and sat on the edge of the bed listening to someone on the phone. He buried his head in his hands. I sat up between him and Allison, waiting. Finally, Dad lifted his head and spoke to the person on the phone.

"Okay, thank you."

He hung up and didn't take much time to breathe or think about it. He was calm.

"Mom died."

I instantly started bawling. I didn't want to believe I was never going to see her again. The pain was immediate. I couldn't stop crying. My poor sick mother, and now dead. I didn't think she was going to die. She'd been gone from us so long in the hospital, but I felt hope she would be back with us again. I kept crying. Allison was almost stoic and told me I shouldn't be crying because I didn't even understand what was happening, like I was too young to grasp the magnitude of our mother's death. That was clearly bullshit. I understood people died and that our mother could die. I knew this was real. I was seven, not an idiot. I wailed.

"I understand!"

Dad was almost as stoic, in a strange state between acceptance and denial. The first thing he did was call Aunt Barbara. Dad said he would tell my brother in the morning. I had pictured Steve sleeping soundly in his bed, oblivious to the pain about to come his way. I felt sorry for him, but envious at the same time.

Donna was buried two days later according to Jewish tradition at Mount Sinai Cemetery in the Hollywood Hills.

A dark cloud fell over our family after that. We were in a state of shock. Dad walked around like a silent, empty shell of himself. He hardly even spoke on the phone and spent a lot of time in the garage. I sat on my bed a lot, not doing anything. I didn't see Allison much as she spent time with her friend around the corner. Steve rearranged his bedroom and kept his door closed. We were a family that talked to each other and argued over trivial things as well as life's hardships. We knew each other's friends and what bothered each other. Normally, Dad kissed us every day and told us he loved us. But now I felt alone, a strange, unpleasant, and foreign feeling.

At the funeral, everyone was dressed in black and stared at me, whispering, probably thinking what a poor, poor child I was, which was true. The pity was unbearable. Sympathies from the women in my family bothered me most. I loved my aunts and cousins, but they always wanted to sit and talk to me about the pretty dress I was wearing or the casserole I was going to love or other things that bored me. I was the girl that hung out with boys because they played sports nonstop the way I liked and were less dramatic.

At the reception, Aunt Sandra sat close to me. I was so angry and bent out of shape. I wanted her to go away. I could barely stand the feel of her pressed against my skin. But she wanted to comfort me and to ease my pain and confusion. I had spent a lot of time with Aunt Sandra and knew she loved me very much. She kept touching me and tried to run her fingers through my hair. I must have stopped brushing my hair by then because her wedding ring snagged and pulled a clump of my hair out with it. It stung, but I didn't care. The pain was almost welcomed. If my mom could go through what she did and die from it, then feeling physical pain somehow made me feel closer to her.

My uncles were easier to handle. Mom's brother Earl, still teary eyed, squeezed my shoulder and moved on, while Uncle Willy patted me on the head and tried to make small talk about the LA Dodgers because he knew I loved that team. Meanwhile, all I thought about was how I was the only kid I knew, other than my brother and sister, who didn't have a mother. It felt all wrong and pissed me off. I hated that my dad was in so much pain and that my brother and sister were so sad. I hated that my mom's life was cut so short and that she died a long, painful death.

It seemed like I hated everything about life. My emotions were almost unbearable and there was nothing to stop my rage. I kept hearing that time would ease the pain and help my dad. I just wanted the sadness to stop.

4

The Baha'is and a Pissed Off Little Girl

The first few days after Mom was gone, people I'd never seen before came over to visit Dad. They brought casseroles and strange food baskets and seemed nice and peaceful. I found out they were the Baha'is checking to see if Dad was okay.

The Baha'is came into our lives because of Dad's second cousin Chuck. We called him Uncle Chuck, and after Mom was gone he was always around. He was a thin man, with caved in cheeks and a thin, dusky mustache. He talked with an East Coast accent, smoked constantly, and drove a yellow cab. He told me stories about his experiences, how he was robbed at gunpoint three times, and twice he was stuffed into the trunk of his cab and left for hours. I couldn't believe Uncle Chuck kept driving a cab when it seemed so dangerous. I used to think he was a brave man.

Uncle Chuck was Jewish but had converted to the Baha'is faith after he moved to California. He told Dad it was the best thing that ever happened to him. Soon, Dad started to feel the same way, and it was the Baha'ises who were kind and nurturing during the worst time of his life. Then just like Uncle Chuck, Dad was no longer a Jew but a Bahai.

He started going to their meetings every week. Since I was still little, Dad insisted I come along with him. I wasn't thrilled about going to a religious meeting, which sounded completely boring.

Not only that, Allison and Steve attended just once and never again. Allison always claimed to have homework, while Steve was always hanging out with his teenage friends. To me, though, it didn't seem fair, and I felt jealous.

One time, the living room at the meeting house was so packed with adults and kids, Dad and I sat on the carpet. I listened to them talk about a man named Baha'u'llah, a messenger of God who was enslaved much of his life but still preached a message of love and equality. Baha'u'llah had millions of followers and was a great prophet like Moses, who I'd only heard of in *The Ten Commandments*, along with the prophet Muhammad.

The times I spent there with Dad weren't too bad. Before they excused us kids to eat cookies and drink punch, they sang pleasant songs, and it was all a pretty good vibe. Dad came to love Baha'u'llah in the same way he said that Christians love Jesus Christ. He was convinced that the Baha'i faith was the way to go. Over the years, whenever the subject of religion came up, Dad always proclaimed his Baha'is faith.

He made all kinds of friends among the Baha'is, famous ones too. Later, Dad brought Alex "Bo" Rocco to our house, the actor, who played Moe Greene in *The Godfather*, a movie Dad and I watched twice. Bo was a likable man and showed me some chords on my guitar, which made me feel special. Another time, Dad brought me to see Seals and Crofts, who I loved, and I was starstruck when we got to go up to the stage and talk to them.

One night, driving home from a meeting, Dad told me that Baha'is believe there are tests given to us throughout our life.

"Mom dying was a test for us. Everyone suffers, Tracy. It makes us closer to God."

What he was saying didn't sound right to me. Why would God, who is supposedly good, take away my mother? So that we will suffer to feel closer to him? If that was true, then such a god was mean and selfish. I felt sad and angry. Religion seemed confusing, unappealing, and even vindictive. I didn't want to talk about God anymore. I was so mad I didn't want to talk about anything. I stayed silent, hoping Dad wouldn't bring it up again.

Uncle Chuck helped Dad connect with his new faith, but he also got Dad to take up smoking cigarettes. For a long time, he sucked on those things and stunk up the house just like Uncle Chuck. It was baffling to me. Dad had no style and seemed awkward smoking them. Whenever he took a drag, his mouth opened when he inhaled, and you could see the smoke filling his mouth. It was gross, and I could tell he really didn't like it very much.

Soon after, *Playboy* magazines started accumulating around the house. Uncle Chuck sometimes sat perusing them at the kitchen table. One time, when just the two of us were sitting there, he turned a magazine to me and pointed at the centerfold's pubic region.

"I don't like this one very much. She's got too much hair down there."

I looked at the lady spread out with her large, perfectly round breasts. Then I glared at Uncle Chuck thinking he was some kind of pervert. I wasn't sure if he had done anything wrong, but I didn't like talking about that with him.

After that, I hid the magazines whenever possible. The last thing I wanted was my brother's friends, or anyone else, rifling through those things. It didn't seem right and was embarrassing.

After three weeks away, I returned to school as a disoriented second grader, still a year younger than my classmates on the outside, but way older inside. I hardly brushed my hair. My clothes rarely matched like they did when Mom was alive, and over a short period of time, I turned into the roughest toughest tomboy in town. All I cared about was playing sports. They were distractions from my melancholy. I constantly played kickball, flag football, and basketball. If I wasn't at school playing sports, I was home playing with neighbors or just by myself. I'd go over to the school yard into the evening, shooting hoops or bouncing a baseball against a paddle board wall and catching it with my glove.

I didn't talk about my mom dying to anyone. It was something we dealt with on our own. Dad was caught up with the Baha'is and tried not to think about Mom. Some of my friends, like my neighbor Kelly next door, or Mark across the street, made extra efforts to spend time with me, showing amazing love and compassion. Their friendship was beautiful, and I will never forget them for that.

Even so, I felt alone. I had trouble verbalizing what I was going through. I knew everyone suffered. But everything felt so broken and unfair, not just for me but for the whole world. My natural tendency was to become increasingly angry. Those first few months I was in a constant funk. Kids laughing or singing bothered me. Things that I thought were unjust or stupid made my blood boil, like rules teachers made in class. I rarely smiled. Strangers noticed my scowl and told me to smile. That only made me angrier. *Mind your own fucking business!* Who were they to tell me how to look or how to feel?

I didn't do well in school any longer. It felt like I'd lost the ability to care.

My third-grade teacher, Mrs. Smith, had stark white hair and must have been the oldest teacher in school. She decided to separate the class into two reading groups, one for the smarter, advanced kids, and one for the slower, seemingly stupid kids. I was put in the slow group. That bothered me a lot. Those other kids weren't smarter than me. I wasn't a bad reader. Couldn't she see I was just distracted? My mother was dead. I just needed a little guidance, maybe some extra encouragement. She added pain to my injury.

I got so mad about the arrangement I stopped talking to Mrs. Smith for the rest of the school year. To me, she was a bad teacher, untrustworthy, and needed to be kept at arm's-length. I couldn't tell if she noticed or cared about the silent treatment. This is when I began to question adult authority and became a problem child. In class and on the playground, I became a strange little enforcer, lashing out at anyone with poor sportsmanship on the field or talking crass to me or my friends.

I didn't mince words much when I came in conflict with others. My instinct was to kick their ass or just use my physical confidence to intimidate them, hoping they'd reconsider and make nice. I was strong for an average-size girl. I'd wrestled and rough housed with my big brother and knew how to throw a punch. But now I was no longer just play fighting; I was angry at the world. That feeling lingered for the longest time. I wasn't a bully as far as I could see, and if you asked my old classmates, I think most of them would have said I was a bully beater. At a recent class reunion, one classmate told me I was the person you wanted on your side.

"You didn't take crap from anyone, Tracy."

I was so ferocious that during recess in the fifth grade I got into a nasty fistfight with a bigger kid named Scott. He called me "big nose" when I passed him at first base during a kickball game. The second I heard those words I stopped. No one called me big nose without regretting it. When I walked back to him and he just stood there, sneering at me, I instinctively took a swing that landed square on his left ear. I knew it stung him big time. I could see tears well in his eyes and his face twisted like he was going to cry.

It felt good to inflict pain on that kid. Scott could be a bully on the playground, and I thought he deserved it. But big Scott wasn't going to let that go. He didn't mind hitting girls as much as I didn't mind hitting boys. Squaring me up, he took a swing at my face. But he was slow and only brushed my chin. Then our confrontation turned into a brawl. Kids on the playground gathered to watch. No one was around to stop us. I don't recall all the punches and swings, but Scott's bottom lip was bleeding, the knuckles of my right hand hurt, and the fight wasn't over when we got back into our classroom.

When we entered our classroom, Scott turned to me and said "big nose" again. I looked up and saw his sneer. Furious, I jumped on him like I was tackling a running back on a football field and toppled him to the ground with my arms wrapped around his head. The teacher's metal desk was right beside us, so I banged Scott's head against it. I was crazed. Classmates cheered us on. It was a spectacle few would forget. Years later, when I saw my best friend, Mark Hillis after more than twenty years, that fight was one of the first things he mentioned.

I kept banging Scott's big head against the desk until Mr. Day grabbed me. His voice was nasally. He punished us by making us write ten thousand times, *I will not talk unnecessarily in the classroom*. I developed a callus on my right middle finger that reminded me to flip Mr. Day the bird whenever his back was turned. He also forced certain misfit kids (myself not included for some reason) to sit with their desks in a long, open-door closet, as far away from him as possible.

Mr. Day took Scott and me to the principal's office, where we spent the rest of the day, separated like animals. Luckily, Principal Stevens felt sorry for me. Over the years, many of my teachers and principals felt the same way. I was a pretty pathetic and sorrowful girl, but they seemed to notice that I had something worthwhile to nurture. I wasn't completely a bad kid.

That day, they called Dad and told him what happened.

"She can sure stand up for herself, but I have another kid that's pretty shaken up."

When Dad showed up to take me home, Mr. Stevens had a short talk with us, telling me fighting wouldn't be tolerated and that I needed to keep my cool and use words—not fists— to stand up for myself. When it was time to go, he patted me on the shoulder and nodded to his secretary.

"Let's give Tracy one of those cupcakes you brought."

Dad didn't consider scolding me for fighting or for throwing the first punch. He just scooted me home and seemed proud. I wasn't in trouble.

After Mom was gone, I was on my own to deal with most of my problems. Dad didn't provide me much guidance. He was already in his own little world, working on vacuums, hanging with the Baha'is, and it seemed like he had bigger problems than me. Allison and Steve weren't helping either. They were grades ahead of me and didn't pay attention to what was going on with their little sister.

Eventually, I began to adjust to Mom being gone, and Dad began to fill the dark void that the three of us kids so desperately felt. I did a little better in school, got into fewer fights, and played lots of sports as well as a little acoustic guitar. It would take far longer for Dad to get used to the idea that he was a single man raising three young kids on his own.

5

What's Elvira Doing in Our Pool House?

We rarely did anything as a family anymore, nothing fun, like going out to dinner or playing board games or going bowling. I was home alone a lot. Dad was no longer carefree, telling jokes the way he usually did. When summer came, days by the pool were far less joyful and family oriented. All Dad wanted to do was sunbathe. It was a lonely time around the house. None of us were happy, but Dad was the saddest of us all.

He constantly worked on the house, on vacuums, and on anything he could get his hands on. He didn't dare slow down. When he wasn't working on those things, he worked on his body. Dad loved bodybuilding and worked relentlessly to sculpt his physique. Bodybuilding was Dad's only sport, other than bowling. He had been weightlifting all his life. When he was nineteen, he won second place in the Mr. Michigan contest. After Mom died, it didn't seem like a day went by without hearing his barbells jingling in the backyard. He did lunges and push-ups with barbells nestled in the small of his back. He did bench presses, arm curls, and sit ups. He had always been fit, but for the first couple years after Mom died, Dad's body transformed into the physique of his youth.

Bodybuilding and his vacuum business weren't enough of a distraction. Coming home to the house was still a constant reminder of my mother and the life they had planned. Dad became depressed the moment he rolled into the driveway. Uncle Chuck once suggested he look for another house, but Dad never considered that. He knew time passing would make our lives better and that someday the misery would subside. But he needed to find a way to cope, so over the months that followed, our house was transformed into something far different than we had ever imagined.

On our housekeeper's last day, Dad had her empty Mom's side of the closet and took everything to Goodwill. He told Allison and I to take what we wanted.

"I can't look at Mom's clothes every day. It makes me sad."

It made me sick to my stomach to think about all of Mom's things leaving the house. I didn't have much interest in her clothes, but Allison kept a few of her favorite dresses. I liked that she did. At least not all of Mom was vanishing. I also took comfort knowing her jewelry was still on their dresser in her jewelry box.

One day soon after, I came home from school to find Dad gutting his closet, spreading everything on the floor and across the bed. I pushed aside a pile of his shirts and sat to watch him for a while. He was pouring baby blue paint into a tray and priming his brush. He planned to build new shelves in the closet and move the movie projector and family film reels into storage. *Out of sight, out of mind* must have been his thinking.

I started dredging through a big box of film reels on the floor. Trips to Las Vegas, Palm Springs, a variety of birthday parties, and Disneyland. Dad loved filming movies of our family adventures. He had Super 8 Kodachrome film developed in the lab. Then, with his action film splicer, he would spend hours editing and splicing the footage. We used to spend evenings watching Dad's movies together on his big rotary movie screen. I always thought it was sad after Mom was gone that we never watched home movies again. Dad didn't film another event of mine until seven years later at my ninth-grade graduation.

That first summer without Mom, Dad took us to weekend swap meets. We weren't looking for any old junk. Dad wanted vacuums, and not just any old ones.

"I want you kids looking for Hoovers, Eurekas, and the Electrolux."

Those were the best built, and Dad wanted as many as possible to keep him busy. Another reason was money. Dad was an economical man and drove a hard bargain with folks selling their vacuums. Sometimes, he got beat-up vacuums for five dollars each and turned them around for fifty dollars or more.

Sometimes, Dad had us split up at the bigger swap meets, like in Simi Valley, to cover as much ground as possible. One time, I spotted a red Royal Classic made of stainless steel, which I knew was valuable. The sticker said five dollars, so I hurried over to Dad to show him. He handed the guy the money with no questions asked and walked away with a huge smile. It was a great feeling when Dad liked a vacuum I found. All I ever wanted was for him to be happy. Sometimes, we came home with a half dozen vacuums and when Dad was happy, we were all happy, too.

Dad kept us kids busy with chores. Steve mostly just took out the trash. Allison did most of the work, taking care of the kitchen and bathroom and shopping for groceries with Dad. I had to do my own laundry, make my bed, and vacuum the carpet twice a week, whether it needed it or not. If I didn't, Dad hunted me down and yelled at me.

"Get your ass in there and vacuum, goddammit."

He was fierce when we didn't do as instructed. I never felt so worthless and ashamed as when Dad was mad at me. So, I learned to do my chores.

Once the vacuum buying fetish subsided and the closet was done, Dad moved on to the pool dressing room. It had a toilet, space to change and was half filled with junk. Dad cleared everything out, vacuumed and mopped the floor, then painted it brick red.

One day, I came home from school and heard a strange banging coming, different from the usual sounds from fixing vacuum cleaners. I skipped opening the refrigerator and made a beeline for the backyard and found Dad fastening a piece of jewelry to a huge poster of a psychedelic gypsy woman on the dressing room wall.

"What do you think?"

Dad's artistic bug had emerged. I couldn't believe what I was seeing. The gypsy poster was an enlarged photograph of a woman who looked like TV's Elvira, lying on her side looking at the camera seductively. She was fully dressed in flowing lingerie and Dad had tacked up Mom's old jewelry to the poster. A beaded necklace hung around the lady's neck, and glistening stones were glued to her fingers. A pair of Mom's earrings were pegged to her ears. All sorts of other posters were covering the walls, too.

Dad trailed me, taking in his handy work. One that caught my eye was the silhouette images of a man and woman in a dozen sex positions, one for each month of the year. They were contorted in all sorts of ways. I couldn't help but stare. I was eight at the time and had some ideas of what sex was, but I never fathomed you could do it in so many ways. With Dad standing there, looking over my shoulder, I felt embarrassed. When I looked at the other wall, I saw a large cartoonish poster of what looked like Adam and Eve standing in a plush garden with their hands on one another's genitals. A detailed serpent-like creature seemed to slither in a tree above them.

"Dad, where did you get all these?"

The poster art wasn't Dad's photography or his own works of art, but the fresh display made the room feel like a miniature art museum. *Awesome!* I couldn't wait to show my friends.

When the first Christmas season without Mom arrived, it felt like it brought a new wave of sadness back into the house. Dad wore that old tight and distant expression, and I could tell he was more distressed than he had been during the previous few months. Everyone knew how much Dad loved Mom, and Christmas exacerbated the pain of losing her.

We were officially Jewish, but Mom never cared about the religious details. She was never a church goer, but she loved Christmas. She had made the house come alive with decorations and the wafting scent of cakes and gingerbread. We always got a tree, Dad always put lights on the house, and we gave each other presents on Christmas morning. Who cared if we had Jewish blood flowing through our veins? For us, Christmas had nothing to do with religion. It was about being together as a family and exchanging gifts.

That dismal year, we got a Christmas tree and decorated it as a family without our mother as best we could. After the holidays, though, Dad had something entirely different in mind for decorating the house.

6

Tile, Anyone?

Dad always loved the look of tile. When my parents took a trip to Tijuana, they brought home a ceramic tiled coffee table with a motif of an ocean wave, which was the prettiest table in our house. So it wasn't a complete surprise when he came home one day with boxes of ceramic tiles. He was so excited about his new project as he explained how cultures across the globe used tile to decorate for centuries.

"Tile is one of man's greatest wonders of the world."

I had to agree; it was pretty cool. Tile was versatile and sturdy and endured the test of time. It held up to moisture and heat, and most important, the designs you could create were endless. Dad was still looking for ways to occupy his mind, and tiling the entire house was his next best idea.

That same day, Dad covered the archway to the dining room with deep blue tile that had gold crescents in each segment. I told him it looked beautiful—because it did! The tile looked perfectly placed, as if a professional had done the work. I could hardly believe how cool Dad made it look. It was rich with depth and the shining glaze caught your eye.

The grouting came two days later, which signaled my turn to help. I watched Dad mix the grout with water, scoop it up with a trowel and press it around the tile. Sponging off the excess grout was the last step. My job was to rinse the black grout out of the sponges and give them back to him.

"Wash them out real good, Tracy."

It was fun to play in the black grout water. The area we were doing was large and covered the lower half of the wall and bordered the archway. When we finished, the tile looked decadent and more attractive with the grout. Dad fell in love with it.

He spun into a tiling madness after that. He tiled the bathroom floor and the countertop. He tiled the windowsills in all the bedrooms and the kitchen. He tiled doorways and cabinet shelves. He tiled through the winter and kept going into spring. Every week he was at the tile store, buying new tile designs.

"Dad, are you going to tile the outside, too?"

I liked it. But would it ever stop?

"There's no telling, girlies."

He was joking, I think, except he had become the go-go gadget tiling man. He found a special satisfaction in the work, which became the exact release he needed to feel better.

Beyond decorating with tile, he accented the hallway walls by covering them from floor to ceiling with square-foot mirrors. He also invested in statues, unusual sculptures, custom paintings, antique swords, and blown glass pieces. Our house felt more like one of the far-out museums you'd find on Hollywood Boulevard, or like the Fun House at the LA County fair than our simple family home.

I had never seen a house decorated like ours. At first, it made me uncomfortable to bring friends over because it seemed so strange. Instead, they were in awe of Dad's tiling handiwork. They bragged to other people about how cool my house was, so maybe he didn't make us look as crazy as I thought. Maybe he was cool, after all.

On the other hand, Dad had a raging temper, which seemed to kick in after Mom died. When I was with him at the vacuum store one day, I heard him talking to Uncle Willy.

"I feel lost without Donna. Sometimes, I feel like I'm going to explode just thinking about it."

Uncle Willy listened to Dad, but talking about his loss provided little comfort; Dad rarely talked about it. He would reach up and press at his eyes, as if talking about it gave him a headache. Then he would change the subject. "Let's have a look at that Electrolux that's been giving you trouble."

If only it was that easy. Anger had a hold on Dad, and it seemed like he was madder at God than anything else. It was always "goddamn" this, and "goddamn" that. It became normal to hear Dad in the garage cussing up a storm. He got mad at the smallest things, whether it was an uncooperative vacuum or slamming his finger on something. His mouth became so foul that it would sting your ears and make your heart skip a beat. I didn't want him to feel bad, but his cursing and frustration scared me, and everyone else. It was embarrassing when I had a friend over and we'd hear Dad go off on one of his tantrums.

One day, when I was in the fifth grade, Jeannie was over after school. We were sitting on my bed talking about a flag football game we'd played. Our team was part of the Burbank Powder Puff league, the greatest thing ever for girls in competitive sports, and our team was pretty good.

As we talked, I could hear Dad in the background working in the garage. I was usually able to tune out the noise, but Dad was extra animated that day. He was pacing by the house with his shoes clicking rhythmically on the cement like they always did. A few minutes later, I heard him talking on the garage phone. Then I heard him banging on something. I turned back to Jeanie who was talking about a play we made that led to a touchdown when suddenly we heard a crash, followed by the sound of breaking glass. Dad started cursing at the top of his lungs.

"God damn, mother fucking, cock sucking, son of a bitch . . ."

That was a common chain of curse words for Dad.

Jeannie looked at me wide eyed.

"Who was that?"

"That's my Dad."

I shook my head and looked at my bedspread.

"He's always throwing conniption fits."

I was afraid Jeannie would never want to come over again. Dad didn't care if the whole neighborhood heard his tirades which they certainly did.

He never lost his temper with any individual. It was usually while he was alone, probably feeling all the mounting frustrations he endured.

After that, whenever I had a friend over I turned on music, which was probably a good thing anyway. Music was soothing to the soul. I hoped it might even soothe Dad. It was either that or I had to play down the street at someone else's house. You never knew what might happen with Dad storming around the garage or the house.

In those moments I wished Dad would have stopped swearing and started tiling. Maybe he could have put tiles on top of tiles until his soul was at peace.

7

Parent Without a Partner

When Mom was alive, we went to Tijuana every year. All of us enjoyed those days in Mexico, eating street tacos and mangos on a stick. Mom and Dad especially liked the great deals you could get on dishes, vases, and beautiful paintings. Tijuana was exotic. Plus, it was only two hours away.

Two years after Mom was gone, Dad decided it was time to take us to Tijuana again. We happily drove down on a Friday evening and rented a motel room in San Diego. Staying overnight just north of the border was how everyone did it. Dad said it was convenient and safe and he didn't have to worry about speaking Spanish as much. On Saturday morning, we got in a short line to drive across the border. Once we pulled up to a small booth, Dad took over.

"Buenos dias, señor."

Dad loved showing off the little Spanish he knew. The guard looked at us in the car and waved us through as if he couldn't care less who came into his country.

Once we got to downtown Tijuana, Dad led us along the dusty streets filled with open air shops, restaurants, and mariachi music. We all loved shopping for souvenirs and Dad gave us all plenty of pesos. He told us to get the best deals we could and to never accept the asking price.

"The Mexicans love to barter."

Counting to ten was all the Spanish any of us knew, but we did our best. Allison bought clothes and art supplies. Dad looked for custom knit shirts or knick-knacks to decorate the house. Steve and I zeroed in on T-shirts and bought mega packs of firecrackers and bigger explosives, like M-40's and M-80's, the kind you couldn't buy in California.

We stopped for lunch at a taco stand, and when I took a bite I thought I was in Heaven. The street tacos were the most amazing food I'd ever tasted. Dad could see how much I enjoyed it too.

"You want another one? I'll get you another one."

He bought us all another round without waiting for our answer.

On that trip, I noticed people staring at Dad, even though he had been working on his appearance most of his life. Even there, where his tan made him as dark as the Mexicans, Dad looked like a foreigner. He had a dark bald head, big black sideburns, and a black handlebar mustache. He wore white shorts with black dress shoes and black socks. Gold jewelry hung around his neck, and he had rings on most of his fingers.

During the two days we were there, he wore bright flowery shirts with the buttons undone to his navel; you could see his dark muscled chest and his well-defined abs. Dad walked tall and radiated self-confidence. If not for a brood of kids tagging along, people may have thought he was the leader of a rock band or a movie star.

When we stopped to take a picture with a donkey and his cart, a Tijuana tradition when Mom was alive, a small crowd gathered to watch Dad. The Mexicans weren't bashful with their stares. It never bothered Dad either. He seemed to thrive on the attention. I found it annoying.

It didn't seem too long after we returned from that trip that I started noticing Dad become more alert when we ran into women around town. He struck up conversations with bank tellers and tried to make the cashiers at the grocery store laugh. One day, while standing in line at Gelson's, the lady cashier caught Dad's eye and he couldn't help commenting to me.

"She's attractive."

I thought Dad would eventually need a woman in his life. Raising us on his own wasn't going to be enough to fulfill him. I could tell he really liked women and enjoyed their company. After Mom died, Dad resisted meeting other women for almost three years. Uncle Chuck had tried to get him out on double dates with him and his girlfriend. But Dad preferred laying tile or hanging posters. He wasn't ready to be with any woman who wasn't my mother.

One day, though, for whatever reason, Dad decided to try the social group, Parents Without Partners. Dad had seen advertisements for PWP in the newspaper. He knew it would be a good place to meet people. His encounters at PWP would soon change Dad's life forever . . . and mine, too.

One Saturday, the four of us loaded into Dad's 1969 Buick Riviera for a picnic with the PWP. It turned out to be the best day trip we'd had since Mom was alive. We all met all sorts of adults and kids. There were pony rides and yard games. I ran the three-legged race with Dad and the two of us tumbled to the ground at the finish line, just like in the Tide detergent commercial I'd seen on TV. I couldn't believe it; people really did fall down at the finish line while running that race. Dad may have been thinking the same thing because we laid there on the ground laughing our heads off. We hadn't done that in a long time.

PWP was a great group for our whole family. They had picnics, bowling parties, and roller-skating nights. All you needed was to be a single parent, a status Dad finally came to grips with. He was getting on with his life. Before long, Dad started seeing less of the Baha'is and more of the PWP people.

He started going out dancing with PWP. He played shuffleboard sometimes and bowled with them. One night at a pool hall outing, the inevitable happened. Dad met a woman he liked. In fact, over the next ten years, Dad would meet five women at PWP that he liked enough to be his girlfriend.

His first encounter was with Joyce, who he didn't date for long, which was perfectly fine with me. He went on a couple of dinner dates with her, and decided he liked her enough to bring her over to the house to meet us. She was soft spoken, well dressed, and worked as a retail saleswoman at JC Penny's in downtown Burbank.

"So nice to meet you."

Joyce smiled and told me she wanted me to meet her two children, who were practically the same age. I felt unsure of this new lady in our house, but she seemed nice enough.

It felt strange to see Dad standing there with another woman, like they were *together*. Dad seemed nervous and kept smiling at her, like he was in awe. I couldn't help but compare her to Mom. Joyce was fairly short, with short brown hair that clung to her neck; she was overweight with a pretty large backside. When I thought about it, Joyce seemed the opposite of Mom, who was above average height, with big, light hair, and was thin. Mom's eyes were blue, and Joyce's were brown. What was Dad thinking?

From the start, the whole girlfriend world of Dad's was confusing. I wasn't sure I liked what was happening. I wanted *my* mother to be with *my* dad. Not this other woman. But I knew thinking like that was a fantasy. Mom was never coming back. I needed to make the best of it.

Joyce was nice to me. Dad and I went to her place, and she cooked us a meal and insisted that I eat as much as I wanted. She poured me and her kids tall glasses of milk and served us bowls of salad. I spent time with her kids after dinner. Her daughter always wanted to play Barbie, and her son just sat there reading a book. I didn't like Barbies, and reading a book wasn't social; it was rude. I ended up hating it over there.

On those visits, Dad and Joyce sat on her front porch holding hands and drinking wine while I waited to go home. I didn't like the way Joyce stroked Dad's arm and kissed him when they said goodbye. The sight of it made me quiver. I worried that she'd try to mother me the way she mothered her own children.

I decided somewhere along the way that no one in the world could ever replace my mother. And if Dad ever got serious and wanted a new wife, that was his choice. But I'd be damned if I would ever call her Mom.

As it turned out, Dad dated Joyce long enough for her to try and mother me when I got bit by a dog.

8

Mark, the Dog Bite, and a Missing Girlfriend

Our neighborhood had lots of kids my age. Kelly, the girl next door to us, loved to play Barbie with her neighbor Christine. I got along with them and was always invited to play along. But the idea of playing make-believe with dolls in a playhouse made me want to puke. If I was going to do anything remotely girlie, it had to be something like crushing rose petals to make perfume or try on my sister's high heels to see what I looked like. That was the extent of my femininity. I played almost exclusively with Mark Hillis, the boy across the street.

We both lived in our houses all our lives, but we didn't start playing together until we were in kindergarten class together. Then, for some wacky reason, I started sneaking across the street so I could blindside him by tackling him on his front lawn. Mark's mom witnessed the assaults through her kitchen window.

"You were a terror to poor little Mark."

She told the same story on a number of occasions.

"Mark would be minding his own business, playing with his ball in the front yard, then you would come along from behind and tackle him to the ground and then you'd walk off like nothing happened."

That was the beginning of a beautiful friendship.

If I had a savior back in those days, I would have to say it was Mark in every way. He was like my twin brother. We did nearly everything together. The days after Mom died, Mark knocked on the back door to see if I could come out and play. He felt bad for me and wanted me to be happy again. He turned out to be the truest friend I ever had.

Mark looked like an all-American kid. He had big, beautiful blue eyes with long dark eyelashes that he once cut off after some lady at the store commented about them. It took weeks for them to grow back. Mark was a complete jock, too. He played every sport I cared about, and he loved to play tackle football on the Burbank Vikings football team. I loved to help him practice.

We'd spend hours throwing a football and running plays on the grass next to our school. Mark was also adventurous the way I liked to be. We were always climbing trees and hopping fences or riding our bikes around town, exploring parks and back city hills. We also just chilled out together. We'd watch our favorite TV shows or play boardgames on cold rainy days.

In the summer, Mark and I became fish and played constantly in our pool. The day I got bitten by a dog, we had spent hours in the water. Dad had left for the day to see Joyce, leaving Mark and me on our own. Even though I was just age ten, Dad had no problem with me playing around at home by myself with a friend—even in the pool. He had no fear about what could happen. Steve and Allison weren't around that day either. Even if they had been, they wouldn't have supervised us. Dad was lax as a parent could be and had no clue how to manage us kids. The odds were good, I suppose, that Mark and I would make it through okay; we always had.

That day was blistering hot. We had no air conditioning in our houses, so the pool was calling. We started off playing every game in the book—diving contests, tea party, Marco Polo. Then we played our own games, like Tarzan and Jane. We jumped off the patio roof into the pool a couple times.

Sometimes, on long swim days, if Dad had put too much chlorine in the pool, after nightfall we'd see halos around lighted bulbs and streetlamps. Eventually though, we got tired of the pool games and needed to move on to something else.

By this time, Mark and I had discovered what we called wall walking. Cinder block walls five feet tall and eight inches wide divided most of the yards in our neighborhood. At some point, Steve and his friends started walking on the back wall by the pool and ventured onto the other walls. Naturally, Mark and I had to try it because I copied my brother in almost everything.

That day, I took the lead and Mark followed me in a direction I hadn't taken before. You could see far ahead into the yards around us. Most of them were landscaped and full of groomed trees and beautiful watered grass. Some were dingy, cluttered with junk and dead shrubbery. We saw swing sets, furnished patios, and swimming pools. Birds flew out of trees and sang songs around us. Some dogs barked while others just watched us go by in our swimsuits and sneakers.

Sometimes, the wall became a fence and others had gaps, so we had to jump to the next wall. Some sections had trees in the way, so we had to climb through them to continue. Many houses away, the wall became a wooden fence, and we shuffled across on two-by-fours until we came to a fence we couldn't walk on. We had to jump down and walk across the yard to the next wall if we wanted to continue to the end of the block and on to the park.

I didn't like jumping into somebody's yard. Part of the challenge was never setting foot on the ground. Not only was it a hassle to climb down and back up again, but my brother's friend jumped into a yard once and ended up with a rusty nail through his foot. I was there that day and watched him pull it out, which was horrifying.

The house had shades over the windows and there was no sign of life. A large avocado tree took up half the yard, and everything was quiet. I jumped first and started across the grass. When I was halfway to the next wall, a German Shepherd bounded around the corner and looked me square in the eyes. I froze, instantly terrified. I'd been bitten by a dog when I was a small child and the memory still weighed heavy in my subconscious. I considered trying to sweet talk the dog.

"Hey, puppy."

The dog snarled and showed his big teeth. Then, like a bat out of hell, it came at me full charge. I started running. Mark saw the dog charging, so he quickly jumped back up on the wall. I knew the dog was gaining ground. I leaped up the wall and started to pull myself up, thinking I was in the clear. But the dog caught me. I felt a shearing pain in my right lower butt cheek and heard the sound of my bathing suit bottom ripping in the grip of the dog's mouth. Once on top of the wall, I knew right away it had broken the skin, because it stung badly.

Shaking with adrenaline, I told Mark I needed to head home. We headed for the street to take the sidewalk. When we passed Mark's house, his older sister Janet called Mark to come home. It was just as well. I didn't want him helping me with my butt wound.

When I examined myself in the mirror, I discovered two shallow tooth gouges in my skin, each about a half inch long. It throbbed like mad. All I knew to do was put Merthiolate on it. Dad used to swab our sore throats with the medicine, and he always swore it could kill any germ alive. I didn't know when Dad would be back, so I swabbed it on as best as I could.

As I sat in the kitchen watching TV, Dad came through the back door with Joyce. She headed straight for the bathroom. I must have looked ill because Dad asked me right away what was wrong. I felt embarrassed about the bite and was glad Joyce was in the bathroom. I told him what happened, that a ferocious dog tried to bite my ass off. He didn't want to hear about the details. All he cared about was how to fix my problem and move on.

"Let me have a look at it."

He signaled me to stand up. I lifted my shorts. He was pleased I had already applied Merthiolate.

"We better put a Band-Aid on it."

By the time he got one and began to apply it, Joyce was in the kitchen.

"What happened?"

She came up close behind Dad and focused on my derriere.

"A dog bit her in the kisser."

Dad sounded jovial.

"Good Lord. What kind of dog?"

Since I had a dad who was partly a nudist, I had grown ever so modest. Having a woman like Joyce seeing my naked butt was a dreadful thought. I didn't want her looking at me, and I especially didn't want her touching me. She wasn't my mother.

"We just put a Band-Aid on. It's fine."

I pulled my shorts back down, but Joyce made a fuss, telling Dad how I would need a tetanus shot or maybe rabies, and that the dog would need to be examined. Dad knew all about dog-bite protocol. After I was bit in the face many years before, an all-points bulletin had been put out on the canine assailant. Neighbors, policemen, and animal control scoured the area looking for a scruffy, coarse haired, thirty-pound mutt. Eventually, they found the dog and its owner. The dog didn't have rabies, so I was spared the shots that were notoriously awful. Later, my parents sued the people with the dog. They settled out of court for twenty-five hundred plus money for the plastic surgeon and the medical bills. The money had been put into a trust fund for me and would accumulate into seventy-eight hundred with interest by the time I turned eighteen.

Thankfully, Dad was nonchalant when it came to getting us medical care.

"She'll be fine. Dogs around here don't have rabies."

Joyce stood there shaking her head in disapproval.

"Well, it doesn't seem right."

Dad tilted his head and gave me an inquisitive look toward Joyce. He mussed my hair and smiled.

"You'll be fine, kiddo."

It must have been a month later that I noticed Joyce wasn't coming around anymore. Dad never mentioned her. She just vanished.

9

The Invasion of Elvis and Groucho

Dad spent more and more time lifting weights and improving his appearance. No doubt, Dad was very vain; he was fit and good looking, and he knew it. He often lifted in front of a full-length mirror that hung on the backyard fence. I'd see him out there posing. He never got huge like some bodybuilders, but Dad was tightly packed, well defined, and had bulging muscles in good proportion for his body type. He liked to show us how he could roll his abs like a belly dancer. He got us laughing and giggling so hard. We all loved it when he did that.

Body hair didn't last long on Dad either. He believed like most bodybuilders that a dark tan, smooth bald skin, and a little body oil gave him the best look. Hair interfered with the beauty and texture of finely developed muscles.

About once a week, he went out on the patio and shaved every inch of his body he could reach with his Sears electric clipper. When he wanted his back shaved, he found one of us to do it. I was usually the one because I was around. I didn't mind doing it too much, but it was a pain sometimes, like when it was hot, and Dad was sweaty, and the clippers didn't move smoothly across his back; it took forever. Dad was always appreciative and usually paid me. Once I was done, and I brushed the loose hair off his back, he stopped me before I left.

"Wait a second. Here's three bucks. And don't spend it all in one place."

He said it jokingly, as if he'd just given me a fortune. That's the way Dad was with money. We were lucky in that respect. His vacuum business did well, and he always had cash. He was always looking for a reason to give us some, too. He didn't like the idea of us leaving the house without cash in our pocket. Shaving his back was nice that way, and at least I earned it.

Just because Dad didn't like hair on his body didn't mean he didn't like it on his head. He had been bald for as long as I could remember. All the men on his side of the family were bald. Dad never liked it and thought he looked older than he was. Once Mom was gone and he became a bachelor on the prowl, he decided a hair piece might serve him well.

One day, Dad hollered from the bathroom to have me come look at a hairpiece he had brought home from a wig and toupee expert he'd found in Hollywood. Dad had a stack of hair pieces sitting on the tiled counter and one was sitting on top of his head.

"You're going to wear one of these?" I asked with surprise and a tinge of displeasure.

"Do you like it?"

I could tell by his tone that he was expecting an affirming answer.

He was supposed to wear the toupees around and get comfortable with the one he liked before getting fitted with the permanent hairpiece. He tried on another one and sized it up in the mirror. I didn't know what to make of it.

"Well, what do you think?" he persisted.

"You look like Elvis Presley."

I was being perfectly honest. The funny thing was that all the toupees looked pretty good on him. They almost looked like real hair, too.

By the following week, the wig experts fashioned Dad a hairpiece just to his liking. But the toupee wasn't just something he slapped on in the morning and hung up when he went to bed. This thing was permanent. Surgically applied.

I'll never forget the day he came home and lifted it up to show me the threads suturing it to his scalp. The thick clear sutures looked like fishing line. It was meant to stay on indefinitely. It was horrifying. All sorts of things went through my mind. *Is he going to shampoo the same way normal people wash their hair? What if he gets into a fistfight and someone pulls on it?* I'd been in fights where my hair got pulled. For Dad it would be like having a pierced earring ripped from your ear. Thank God he never got in fistfights.

Dad's facial hair was turning gray, so he started dying everything jet black—mustache, eyebrows, sideburns, and the hair around the sides of his head. On some dye days, he roamed the house looking like Groucho Marx. Sometimes I'd be outside in the front yard playing with a friend and Dad would come out like that to get the mail or water the lawn. *How can he go out in public like that?* It was embarrassing. But Dad didn't care what people thought or if they stared, and I suspect he enjoyed the attention.

Dad really was an interesting looking man. Everyone seemed to think so because they couldn't stop staring, and it happened even more when he got the hairpiece and dye job. One time, Dad and I went to Ralph's for groceries and three people at the entrance stopped to stare at him. I glanced over at him; Dad looked like he always did. He had his shirt unbuttoned down to his belt buckle and his chest was bulging out. He was extra tan with his recent sunbathing. Maybe that was why he was getting so many intense stares. Maybe people really thought he was in the movies and wanted to get a good look at him, to see if they recognized him. Whatever it was, I didn't like the stares and I never got used to it.

I shook it off and followed Dad as he grabbed a cart and headed for the meat section. A lady reaching for some pork chops stopped to stare. Then a young couple in the dairy section froze in their tracks. I couldn't believe how rude they were, being so blatant. I felt like pummeling all of them. Instead, I just glared. By the time we were done, I was infuriated. Dad took it in stride, never fazed about it. He even smiled at some of them.

When I got home, I told Allison. She laughed her head off.

"You are just noticing? Good lord, Tracy. Everyone stares at Dad. Get with it, girl."

10
Ditched at Disney

By 1975, while Dad focused on his vacuum business, dating women, and bodybuilding, our house on Wyoming Avenue became a frenzy of teenage activity. Steve was popular at school and had a trove of friends. The girls who came around the house thought he was a cutie with his big smile, luscious long hair, and magnetic brown eyes. It seemed like everyone in Burbank knew my big brother. I was amazed how often someone spotted me at the park or the mall and asked me if I was Steve Steingold's little sister.

On most weekday mornings, some of Steve's friends would stop at our house to hang out before school. Then they walked to school together. After classes, they came back to our house to hang out for the afternoon. Steve's three best friends were around a lot. Ernie Escovelle, Mark Mancinelli, and John Faber formed a diverse group. Ernie was Mexican, Mark was of Italian descent, John was just White, and Steve was Jewish. The boys wore faded blue jeans, silk screen printed T-shirts and had long wavy hair past their shoulders.

When Steve got his royal blue 1966 Ford Fairlane, the boys sat out in his car and listened to rock and roll with the volume up so loud it vibrated the house windows. I thought they looked silly sitting out there in a parked car, but they were decent boys and usually nice to me. But sometimes they played along when Steve teased or taunted me.

The spring I turned ten, Steve and his best buddies were going to Burbank Nite at Disneyland. The city of Burbank provided buses to Anaheim, and I begged Dad to let me go with the boys.

"Can I go to Burbank night at Disneyland? Can I go? Can I go with Steve?"

Dad liked the idea of me going. Allison was at a friend's house, and Dad was going out on a date that night, and I'd be home alone anyway.

"Sure, you can go."

Dad told Steve I was going with him. Steve looked at me and glared. He couldn't believe what was happening.

"Dad, you really want me to take my little sister to Disneyland with all my friends?"

Dad snapped at Steve the way he often did when his mind was made up and we were pestering him.

"You're taking her, and that's that."

Dad didn't care how his son felt about it. Steve shook his head and walked out of the room without looking at either of us. He was angry with me, but I didn't care. I wanted to go to Disneyland so bad. It didn't matter how bent out of shape my big brother was.

As far back as I can remember, Steve never wanted much to do with me. I was seven years younger than him. Little sisters could be a pain. I got that. One day, when I was standing on top of our back wall, Steve and his friends came through the back gate and saw me there. He was carrying his BB gun and shot me in the leg. It stung sharp in my thigh without breaking the skin. I yelled out in pain. Steve and his friends got a great laugh out of that.

Steve was also mean to me when his friends weren't around. He thought it was entertaining to pin me down and sit on my chest so I couldn't move. He'd just sit there, laughing at me, and sometimes he pretended he was going to spit on me. He'd hock up a big mucous loogie and string it down from his mouth to my face, like a yo-yo. Thankfully, he wasn't malicious and had a knack for sucking the spit up right before it hit my face. I was disgusted *and* grateful. Other times, he held me face down and dug his elbow or his chin into my back. It tickled like the dickens, but sometimes it hurt. I begged him to stop. He wouldn't until I cried "Uncle."

Dad was always gone when Steve picked on me. When Dad was home, squabbles and acts of torture were never tolerated. Dad couldn't stand us arguing and would put a stop to it immediately. I never thought he favored Steve over me, being a boy, or Allison for being older. If anything, I thought he favored me most because I was the youngest. I had my frustrations with Dad for his yelling and cursing and being gone all the time, but I loved him deeply. He may have been an unstable rock, but he was the only rock I had.

The evening I went to Disneyland with my brother, there must've been half a dozen buses at the high school taking Burbank kids to Anaheim. I was excited and giddy. Disneyland was my favorite place in the world. Steve ignored me from the moment we got on the school bus.

Once we reached the park, Steve still hadn't said two words to me. We went on a couple rides in Tomorrowland. When we did the boat ride, Steve got in a boat with his friends and told me to take the next one. I had an entire boat to myself, but I wanted to ride with Steve. I could see them ahead of me, laughing and carrying on. When I got off my boat, the boys were nowhere in sight. All four had vanished.

I looked around, scouring the area, thinking they were joking around and just hiding. But there was no sign of them. I stood there in a state of shock. My brother had ditched me.

I wasn't scared to be alone at Disneyland. I knew how to get back to the buses to get home. I knew even back then that Disneyland was the safest place on Earth. But I can't deny my feelings were badly hurt.

I roamed the park and went on rides for the rest of the night, trying to make the best of it. I kept an eye out for Steve and his friends, but I never saw them until I got on the bus and Steve was in the back, smiling with all his buddies. When he saw me take a seat he came over and squeezed my shoulder.

"Here, I got you this."

Steve handed me a bag of rock candy. I *loved* rock candy.

Steve may have thought that was enough to make up for what he did. But I never completely trusted my big brother after that. In fact, my whole family wasn't all that reliable. The way I was starting to see it, I'd have to figure out a lot of things on my own. I never spoke a word of Steve ditching me to Dad. There was no use making a big deal about it. I did get to go to Disneyland, though, after all, and it felt kind of good to have figured it out on my own.

My dad always loved to be the center of attention and loved bodybuilding. At nineteen, he placed 2nd in the Mr. Michigan contest.

Mom and Dad at the lake. 1950's.

Here's Dad on his Harley. You can see he was even decorating his vehicle back then with extra chrome balls attached around the windshield. 1952.

I'm never so proud of my dad as when I look at this picture of his paratrooper, medic days in the Army. 1946.

Early picture when my mom
was still alive. Look how cute
and innocent we look. 1965.

Here we are living the
California dream. Around
1967

I had many mishaps at a young age. At three, I got bit in the face by a neighborhood dog. I still have the scars.

Dad took countless pictures of me and mom together. This one Is my favorite. Notice how she keeps me off the bottom.

My sister, Allison, in front of
Dad's tiling handy work of
the living room archway, the
fireplace and mantle.

Shirtless, here I am aspiring to
be like my dad and showing an
inclination for the guitar. Looks like
I'm about four here.

Are baby butts allowed
in a book gallery? It
sure looks like it. 1964

11

Queen of the House

Although Allison was still a kid, she tried to be the woman of the house after Mom was gone, and Dad encouraged it.

"I'm going to need some extra help around here."

I was too young, and Steve was a teenage boy. I think Dad figured that if anyone could manage the job it was Allison. She started doing laundry, the shopping, and cooking meals as best she could. She tried cooking cow's tongue like Mom, but no one would eat it, not even Dad, which was a big blow since he ate just about anything you put in front of him.

Most of the time, it was nice that Allison helped the way she did. But sometimes, I hated how she took over the house and bullied me into doing chores.

"I want you to vacuum."

"You need to do your dishes."

"Now!"

For a while, she tried to tell me when I could go out and when I had to be back. She was my big sister—not my mother. I couldn't stand her bossiness. We screamed and yelled when Dad wasn't around, and I called her "fatso" and "thunder thighs." When she tried to grab me, I ran, and she could never catch me.

Allison was growing up so fast that she looked the part, too, in her pretty dresses, high heels, and makeup. Everyone I knew thought she was much older than she was. I was impressed by how she got away with just about anything.

One time, when Dad took us to Las Vegas, Steve and I sat in one row and Dad and Allison were behind us. We were on one of TWA's champagne flights. When the stewardess served drinks, we heard her talk to Dad.

"Would you and your wife like a glass of champagne?"

Steve and I were stunned. Allison was barely fifteen at the time. How could the stewardess possibly think my sister was Dad's wife? Allison was wearing a brown and beige maxi dress down to her ankles, and she was holding a funky stuffed animal. Was the stewardess drinking champagne too? When she brought the champagne, Dad asked if his other two kids could have some. The stewardess shook her head, but Allison kept hers, which aggravated me and Steve.

Around the house, Dad let Allison do just about anything she wanted. Her friends were constantly around, and they often had slumber parties with seances and a Ouija board. Allison didn't mind if I stuck around, and I loved being with older kids. During seances, we all held hands in candlelight, and said the same thing over and over again.

"We would like to contact Bloody Mary . . . Bloody Mary . . ."

Then we'd start laughing because it was so silly.

One summer day, when Allison was sixteen, Dad let her have a party with several cases of beer, and she and her friends all got drunk. Dad didn't buy the alcohol. The liquor stores hardly carded anyone who looked old enough, and Allison surely did. I was just eleven but also had Dad's permission to indulge.

"You better watch out, Tracy. That stuff will grow hair on your chest."

Dad was trying to be funny and didn't mind me drinking beer, so I kept drinking. At first, the beer tasted bad, but the more I drank the better it tasted. I got so drunk I staggered around the living room and felt so silly and fancy free that I did cartwheels and told stupid knock-knock jokes to Allison's best friend, GiGi, who loved my antics. I liked making her laugh. Drunk children are apparently funny, and I wanted to make them laugh more and more.

A tall statue of a Spartan holding a spear stood near the fireplace. The girls watched me as I sauntered over to the man and started kissing his hard, cold lips like I saw people do on TV. Allison's friends cracked up. I pretended to make out with him, until I felt queasy, and the room started spinning. I ran to the bathroom and threw up fourteen times. I counted. I'd never vomited so much in my life and thought it could be a world record.

Besides alcoholic beverages, the house was always full of food. Every week, Dad and Allison filled two grocery carts with six cartons of milk, TV dinners, cereal, steaks, tongues, and anything else we wanted.

Dad bought T-bone steaks by the dozen and packed them in an extra freezer. When I had sleepovers, we cooked them in the broiler in the middle of the night. Dad didn't care.

Dad loved junk food, like beer nuts, Slim Jims, Ding Dongs, M&M's, Hershey bars, Chico sticks, and beef jerky. On the kitchen counter we had two cookie jars, one with Ding Dongs, and the other with Oreos. They were rarely empty.

"Let's go to the Steingolds' and eat Ding Dongs!"

That was a familiar refrain. Our house was popular because we had a pool, endless junk food, and almost no adult supervision. Year after year, long-haired teenagers hung out and ate Dad's junk food, and he didn't care one bit. He was too busy making money, fixing vacuums, and dating his girlfriends. He didn't pay much attention to what went on at home. Kids even smoked pot in the backyard. Even when he was home, Dad wasn't concerned about what anyone was doing. I think he bought junk food just to keep everyone happy.

Things were wild and unconventional, but for the most part we fared pretty well. As the pain of losing Mom faded, we got along okay. Allison included me in a lot of things, and to a certain degree, she looked out for me. Maybe having all those friends over was a way for us to heal and Dad's way to move on. As long as we were happy, Dad didn't care about anything. It wasn't until things started disappearing from the house that he finally woke up.

12

The Thief

I t all started when our Sparkletts bottle with thousands of pennies disappeared from the living room. We had been saving since I was a toddler. A few days after it went missing, Dad found the bottle by the pool, broken into a million pieces. Whoever took the pennies must have brought the bottle to the dressing room, filled their bags and pockets with our pennies, and broke the bottle just to be mean.

Unfortunately, that was just the beginning. Soon after, money went missing from Dad's dresser drawer. A while later, it happened again, and then again. Steve had a big cardboard elephant on the wall of his bedroom where he collected silver dollars, and those started to disappear, too.

One day, Dad called us into his room. We seldom had family meetings, and when we did it meant something was wrong. We sat at the end of his bed as he paced back and forth, obviously angry.

"This stealing has got to stop."

His face heated red as he talked, and none of us dared to utter a word.

"I don't want any of your friends in the house when you're not here."

He was ranting, but everything sounded reasonable. Some of Allison's friends had been letting themselves into the house while waiting for her to come home. Some kids watched TV while we were swimming. Dad was making a lot of sense. But the more he talked, the angrier he got.

"We need to lock the goddamn doors when no one's here."

He waved his arms in a quick jerking motion.

"It's your goddamn friends."

I was in sixth grade, and Dad and I were taking guitar lessons from my teacher, Mrs. Schmidt. We each had an acoustic guitar, which were leaning against a wall in Dad's bedroom. I stared at mine as he talked.

"Just the idea of someone in here going through my dresser. Taking my fucking money."

The next thing I knew, Dad, his eyes wild and fierce, picked up my guitar by the neck, raised it to the ceiling and smashed it to the floor, breaking it into a thousand pieces. I could hardly believe it. How could he do such a thing? If he was going to throw a fit, at least he could have broken his own guitar. I loved mine and had been playing it every day. It was heartbreaking to see it scattered all over the rug. I sat there speechless and boiling mad.

"Geez Dad."

Steve scratched his whiskery chin. At first, I thought he was grinning, but he looked more perplexed than anything. So did Allison, who had her typical reaction.

"Well, Dad, that's not going to help anything."

Tears ran down my face as I bolted to my bedroom. When the anger subsided and my thoughts cleared a little, I came to one conclusion. The thief needed to be stopped. There was no telling what Dad might do the next time. I wasn't sure how we were going to catch whoever it was, but we had to because whoever the thief wasn't finished.

The suspect list wasn't too hard to figure out. Whenever Allison had parties, a neighborhood kid, Frank, often came over. He was Steve's age, tall and heavy set, with beautiful, long golden hair. He wore glasses half an inch thick so when you faced him straight on, his eyes looked magnified to twice their normal size, like he was looking through a Coca Cola bottle. I always felt sorry for Frank and his thick glasses. They had to weigh heavy on the nose and it didn't make him look smart like other people who wore glasses. They made him look dorky.

Frank had problems with his parents and couldn't live with them any longer, so he had moved into a guest house in his grandparents' backyard. He liked to smoke pot and cigarettes and walk around the neighborhood visiting people. Frank could talk to anyone—parents, kids, Allison, and her girlfriends. Dad seemed to enjoy talking to him as well and kept him company in the yard. Dad still smoked cigarettes at the time and Frank usually mooched one and they'd smoke together and shoot the breeze.

We all liked Frank. He was always invited to hang out, and he spent lots of time with Allison and her friends, mostly drinking beer and eating our food, which was especially handy for him since he was often high on weed and had the munchies.

One day, I was alone in the house doing chores when I heard a knock at the back door. My bicycle had been stolen, so I was homebound cleaning up the house and trying to stay out of trouble. I heard another knock and Frank's voice.

"Hello? Ernie? Anybody home?"

The door opened.

"Anybody home?"

I froze, curious to see what Frank would do if he thought no one was home. I was feeling particularly vigilant because the last time Dad got ripped off he called the police. They dusted for fingerprints and talked to him about the thief's pattern. I knew the police could never sort out who it was because too many people came and went.

I was determined to catch the thief myself. I even drew a little diagram of how I was going to do it, like where they might enter the house and where I could hide. In hindsight, it's amazing how well my drawing predicted what actually happened.

I heard Frank creeping down the hallway. Two seconds later, he paused at my doorway and continued toward Dad's bedroom. When I was sure Frank was inside, I tiptoed out in pursuit, planning to catch him red-handed. I saw Frank hovering over Dad's dresser.

"What are you doing in my dad's room, Frank?"

His eyes bugged out behind his thick glasses.

"Looking for a cigarette butt."

There was an ashtray on the dresser filled with half-smoked cigarettes. Dad was always leaving them around because he didn't like smoking them. You could tell by the way he half choked on them.

Frank had thought this through. He picked a butt out of the ashtray and walked past me with a perfect alibi. I couldn't prove anything. I wasn't even sure he was the thief.

"Just stay out of our house."

Just like that, the thief got away. At least that's what I always thought.

When Dad got home, I told him what happened. I was still riled by the image of Frank lurking in the bedroom.

"He could be the thief."

Dad considered the idea. He lay down his clipboard and removed his pocket protector. I followed him into his room where he looked at the ashtray.

"You didn't see him open a drawer or take anything?"

"I wish I did."

Standing in the doorway of his closet, Dad 's pants dropped to the floor as well as his boxer shorts. I saw his private parts hanging there, and I contemplated his nakedness for a moment. It was nothing new. Dad still walked around naked in front of us, so it hardly fazed me. He never thought twice about being naked in front of his own children. It was a perfectly natural state of being for him and there was nothing deviant about it. It was just Dad. All of him.

We had no proof that Frank was stealing, and Dad thought Frank's excuse for being in his bedroom was plausible.

"That kid is always mooching cigarettes."

I couldn't believe Dad's response. I thought he would be angry that Frank was snooping around, or at least be suspicious, but he seemed to fall for Frank's story hook, line, and sinker. "I'm going out for a swim."

He left the room in his black Speedo and rubber thongs.

After that day, Frank hardly came over. I must have scared him. The best part? Money stopped disappearing.

13

Allison Gets Arrested

There is always one kid who gets in trouble at any school, and in my junior high school that was me. Dad offered little direction when it came to my education, and he had little regard for my behavior outside the house. I became a loose cannon and did all sorts of questionable things at school, like sneaking out of class and walking the halls, using foul language, and talking back to teachers I didn't like.

My conflict with authority figures continued because I think I liked the attention, and because I had a bad attitude. At least that's what Allison told me.

"You have a bad attitude, Tracy."

She'd snap at me with disappointment in her voice. I think she was right. I couldn't stand certain teachers, and some of them couldn't stand me. They probably saw me as a kid going nowhere and thought I was a brat. They had no interest in me. That only made me feel more persecuted.

I did like some of my teachers and went the extra mile for the ones I respected, loitering after class to talk to them. Among my favorites was Ms. Giroux, one of my seventh-grade teachers. She was new and stood outside her classroom to greet kids as we came in. I liked the way she looked at me. She asked me questions about myself and seemed genuinely interested. But I still kept teachers, even her, at arms-length. I don't know what I was afraid of because I wanted to be her friend, but I didn't know how. I adored that lady, and I still think about her.

In the eighth grade, Dad was called in for a meeting with my vice principal, Mrs. O'Malley, who I knew well—and liked—from all the times I had been called to her office. Our talks about my behavior were always fair, and her reprimands were never harsh or critical. When I saw her in the hallway, she made a point to smile at me. But for this meeting, I wasn't invited. It was just Dad and my math teacher, Mr. Weber.

Turns out, he wanted me out of his class. Dad said Mr. Weber was very emotional.

"The man turned three shades of red, Tracy. Mr. Weber doesn't like you."

"He said he didn't like me?"

"That's what he said."

I couldn't believe Mr. Weber would admit to such a thing. But I knew it was true. I always felt like he wouldn't give me the time of day. On a couple occasions, I raised my hand to ask a question, but Mr. Weber pretended he didn't see me. He always called on the boys to answer questions. I resented teachers playing favorites. I wasn't a great student, but math was my best subject, and I was getting decent grades.

I hadn't been the nicest person to Mr. Weber, and I made fun of him to my classmates. He was not an attractive man. He had a long, narrow head, his mouth hung open, and he had deep craters all over his face. I knew it was wrong to make fun of someone's looks. I had to deal with plenty of "big nose" remarks throughout my life. But I whispered my insults anyway, and I made them loud enough for him to hear. No wonder he didn't like me. I was awful. But then again, I thought he was awful, too.

Still, I'm not sure what came first, making fun of Mr. Weber or him ignoring me. Either way, our dislike was mutual.

"Well, you're in a different math class now."

"Just like that?"

"Teachers can do anything they want if you act like a brat."

Dad told it to me straight. He didn't worry about me or think about what I was up to. Even when I was in my teens, Dad let me have an incredible amount of freedom. I could be across town with a friend with the sun setting and not be heard from for hours. Dad didn't worry. Steve and Allison could be out all night drinking and smoking pot with their friends, and Dad didn't concern himself. He had this naive trust that we would be okay and do the right thing.

He yelled at us when we didn't do things he told us to, like chores, or for splashing too much water out of the pool. His scolding was often loud and fierce and made me afraid sometimes. I used to cower in my bedroom and clean it especially well when Dad was angry with me. How could I be a bad person if my bedroom was clean? But with all the freedom Dad gave me, it was hard to not get into trouble. That was also true for Allison.

One night, Dad took me with him to the Van Nuys police station because Allison had been arrested for driving under the influence. The police let her into the lobby to talk with Dad. I was scared for her because Dad looked so flaming mad.

"Were you drinking and driving?"

"I only had three beers, Dad."

For a second, I thought he might smack her right there in the police station. He'd been known to do that out of the blue when we really got out of line. But Dad kept his cool.

Lucky for Allison it was a busy night for the police, and they hadn't booked her yet. I noticed Dad take a long look around the station. A few people were seated in the waiting area. Two uniformed policemen stood behind a counter with their backs to us, paying no attention.

Dad looked at Allison with a fierce, vigilant eye.

"Let's go."

Go? Didn't the police want to prosecute my sister? Dad turned and led Allison out the front door. I followed quickly behind.

When I looked back, the police were still talking to each other and completely oblivious.

It wasn't until I was in the car that I realized Dad was larger than life. He had taken Allison out of the police station without permission. She was never charged with DUI.

I sat in the back in disbelief. I didn't know if Dad had broken the law, but it didn't matter. He had guts and I was in awe of him.

14

See You Later

Dad spent most evenings with Parents Without Partners. Wednesday nights meant bowling with his new friends, and when I didn't have anything better to do, I went along to watch.

The Pickwick lanes were a zoo on weeknights. Older men with slicked back hair and women dressed in capris with their hair dolled up milled about between turns. It looked like mating season at the bowling alley. I usually sat in a swivel chair next to the scorekeeper chair. Dad made sure to introduce me to his teammates.

"This here is my youngest."

Dad always changed the way he introduced me.

"Hey Lois, this is my youngest daughter."

"Hey George, come shake my youngest kid's hand."

I couldn't keep the names of Dad's friends straight, but I shook their hands the way Dad told me. "Always look the person in the eye, and none of that limp hand stuff."

Dad could never sit still. After he smashed the pins with his signature torpedo throw, I'd watch him talk to one woman after another. He seemed like a magnet. They all smiled big at him and gently touched his arm with their soft hands. All night long, Dad talked to just about everyone who came within ear shot. He might have been the friendliest, most social person in the bowling alley.

Going out dancing with PWP was Dad's favorite weekend activity. I'd be sitting at the kitchen table watching TV and Dad would come in all dressed up and smelling like British Sterling cologne.

"I'm going dancing tonight. Steaks and TV dinners in the freezer. Don't stay up too late."

I was going on twelve and was used to being home alone. I usually ate junk food and watched my favorite TV shows, like *Sonny and Cher* and *The Brady Bunch*.

Dad was always on the go and my schoolwork was never on his radar, so I didn't have anyone holding me accountable. Consequently, I worked just hard enough to get by so I could play with my friends. I passed with average grades, no thanks to Dad. But I also welcomed not having a parent hounding me about my studies. Some of my friends couldn't leave the house until their homework was done. I was usually free like a bird after I heard what seemed like Dad's favorite phrase.

"See you later."

When I didn't feel like being alone, I went to Mark's and spent the evening there. His parents were the nicest people in the world and never seemed to mind me coming around. I watched TV with all of them, shows like *National Geographic*, *Wild Kingdom*, and college football. Mark's mom offered me cookies or scrambled eggs if that was what she happened to be cooking. Mark's dad, who worked at Lockheed, formulated long-division problems for me and Mark. We loved figuring them out and sometimes begged his dad to formulate more.

Even after dark, Mark and I played silly games outside, like hide-from-cars, or we went trick-or-treating in ghostly bed sheets when it wasn't Halloween. People usually shut their doors in our face, but sometimes we'd score a Hershey bar from an old lady on Avon Street.

At times, we were downright delinquent. We often took off without saying anything to anyone. Nobody had a clue what we were up to. We were the kind of deranged children who took satisfaction in rubbing dish soap across car windshields or ringing someone's doorbell and running off. We didn't need a reason. We just thought it was funny.

Sometimes we stole things. Grace, who lived next to Mark, had a garden full of strawberries. When we thought the coast was clear, we'd jump the fence and pick as many as we could. We probably could have asked Grace, and she would have welcomed us. But we liked stealing them better.

Sometimes we stole things we didn't need at all, like CB antennas or hubcaps. One night, we took a pack of Marlboros off the seat of a pickup truck. Once we got some matches, we lit a cigarette in Mark's backyard playhouse. Two minutes later, we were choking and sick to our stomachs. We never smoked again.

One night, we ventured farther away from home and came across the Pepperidge Farm factory. We saw crates of bread on a platform, waiting to be loaded onto big trucks for delivery.

"Do you smell that bread?"

"Think anyone would notice if we took some?"

We hid behind a wall until the coast was clear.

"Tracy, if you grab some first, I'll get some, too."

That was all the encouragement I needed. I figured if I got caught, I would drop the bread and run. No harm, no foul. With my heart beating double time, I dashed up the stairs to the platform, grabbed two loaves in each hand and ran back behind the wall. We got home with eight loaves of bread. Stealing from Pepperidge Farm went on for weeks, and it's a wonder we didn't get bread poisoning.

When Christmas season arrived, our carousing on the streets of Burbank sunk to a new low. Most houses were covered in lights, so stealing the bulbs seemed exciting. We didn't know why we chose to do it. I guess we were mentally defective. So, we unscrewed hundreds of bulbs and collected them in a grocery bag. I took some home to replenish Dad's supply, but we threw the rest at passing cars to scare the drivers, or we went to school and threw them on the blacktop to hear them pop.

One Christmas, when we were old enough to drive, Mark and I tried stealing trees. We hit the big lots where the poor lonely trees, cut off at the foot, stood in the dark far away from watching eyes. It was easy to drive up to a stand of trees where Mark jumped out, grabbed a tree, threw it in the trunk, hopped back in, and I drove off. The unsuspecting attendants in their trailers never knew what hit them. We stole a bunch of trees that year and gave them to neighbors as gifts, which was the only redeeming thing about our capers. We thought we were like the Robin Hoods of Christmas trees.

We did the same with the bread. The neighbors we liked were stocked with rye, whole wheat, and pumpernickel. Few questions were asked about the bread or the trees. I don't think anyone wanted to know. It's no wonder Mark's sister Janet thought we needed to start reading the Bible. We were clearly bound for Hell.

15

Cheering for God

Janet was eleven years older than Mark and had some mysterious authority over him. She was tall, pretty, athletic, and a master baton twirler who led our high school band and then the UCLA marching band at halftime shows at football games and in parades like the Tournament of Roses. She became a cheerleader for the Los Angeles Rams and eventually got Mark and me tickets to see Vince Ferragamo and the Rams win the NFC wildcard game in 1979.

Before a big game, she warmed up out in the street, dressed in her sequin leotard, wearing Bruin blue fingernail polish and matching eye shadow. The neighbors came out to watch while Mark and I sat on the curb. I loved her practice routines. I was always amazed at how high she could throw the baton and then catch it while she twirled her body so gracefully, like when she did baton helicopter twirls around her legs. It was exhilarating.

Janet was so good that some nights she twirled fire to show off her skill and courage. My heart raced whenever she did that. I'd watch her intently, eyes glued as the flames lit up the dark sky. It was because of Janet that Mark and I chanted the UCLA fight song and hated their rival, USC. She was the spitting image of school pride and hard work and seemed perfect to me in most every way.

She did, however, annoy some people who thought she was the ultimate showoff. Janet was confident and laughed off the criticisms.

"I don't care what those little brats think."

Janet got a kick out of telling me a story about an encounter she had with Steve when he was about ten and she was fifteen. Janet was twirling on the sidewalk, when Steve, riding his bike on the sidewalk, decided to nonchalantly nudge his front wheel into her.

"Hey, watch it," she said.

Without saying a word, Steve kept riding and Janet continued her practice routine. Five minutes later, my brother, still on his bike, bumped into her again. Janet, now angry but willing to forgive, gave him a warning.

"You do that again, you're going to be sorry."

Five minutes later, Steve bumped into her a little harder. Janet raised her baton and smacked Steve hard on his arm. Steve, stinging with pain, rode straight for our house. A few minutes passed before the sound of my dad clearing his throat got Janet's attention. He had pulled up in his old Ford work van next to where she was standing.

"You touch my son again and I'll take that baton and wrap it around your neck."

He nodded, gave her a wink, and drove off.

I laughed hard and loud at that one. Dad was notorious for getting only one side to the story. Janet laughed, too, as she thought about it.

"It's been years, and your dad and I still haven't exchanged two words."

Mark's family didn't attend church as far as I could tell, but Janet must have been a Christian. I sometimes saw her on Sunday mornings, getting into her Chevy Nova, decked out in a pretty dress, holding a Bible under her arm. There was something about the way Janet carried herself that seemed gracious or even reverent. I never once heard her talk about drinking alcohol or going to parties. I couldn't imagine her drinking a beer or smoking pot like my brother and sister. I never heard her curse or talk indignantly about anyone.

One day, Mark's mom saw Mark and I picking and eating strawberries in Grace's yard. She was furious. The trouble didn't last long though. She didn't even tell my dad. Mark's parents never told Dad anything. I liked that about them.

Soon after, Janet called Mark and me into the house to have a talk. She explained that she knew all about the mischief we had been up to, including the strawberries, which was the tip of the iceberg. She told us that if we wanted to play together we had to memorize all the book names of the Bible.

"What?"

Mark was confused. I wasn't sure I heard her right either, but she was dead serious. She wanted us to memorize the names of every book in the Bible.

"Mark, Mom, and Dad aren't going to do anything about you two. The last thing they need is to be picking you up from the police station."

She grabbed a Bible on the table and slid it in front of her.

"If you want to play together, memorize the names of every book."

She was right. We were constantly up to no good. Mark was as much an instigator as me, but knowing that Janet thought I was a bad influence or a bad person made me uncomfortable. I idolized her. In some ways, she made me want to be a better person, and ultimately, I think she had a positive effect on me. I just couldn't believe she had the authority to make us read the Bible. I wanted to tell her to go fly a kite, but I didn't have the courage to speak to her that way. Who knew what she would do? She might have finally had a long talk with Dad. That wouldn't be good. I looked at Mark in disbelief and waited for him to say something.

"So, you want us to do what?"

She opened the Bible, flipped through some pages, and pushed it over to Mark.

"Look, your name is in it."

I scooted closer to have a look for myself. Matthew, Mark, Luke, John. I had never read the Bible. I didn't know anything about it. I remembered asking Dad once who wrote it.

"The prophets and saints."

I didn't understand what that meant but I always thought the Bible was something divine or supernatural, like the word of God.

That day, Janet told us to memorize the names of the first five books of the New Testament. Then, in the second week, all the names of the first ten books. Five more every week until we knew them all. If we didn't memorize every book in sequence, Mark would no longer have permission to play with me.

I had to wonder why Janet chose the books of the Bible. Why not force us to actually read the Scriptures? At least we might have learned something. I figured she was getting a kick out of telling us what to do.

As it turned out, her assignment was kind of fun. Within a month, Mark and I memorized every book's name of the New Testament. After two months, we could recite every book name of the Old Testament, too. We were ahead of schedule. Years later, I could still recite those books by memory.

16

Pickled Onions and Kawasakis

Soon after those Bible book names had been embedded in our brains, Mark and I took a long break from each other. Ironic? Maybe, but that's just the way it was back then when it came to friendships. Easy come. Easy go. We all migrated from friend to friend. I spent a couple weeks with Kathy, a month with Betty, and then back to Kathy.

Most of my friends were kids I knew from Luther Burbank Junior High, which was predominantly white, with pockets of Mexicans, a small group of Russian immigrants, a couple of Black kids, and maybe a dozen Asians. During seventh grade, I spent time with a Korean girl named Paeok (Pay-yoke), who was two years older and lived around the corner. She turned out to be one of my most kind and loyal friends. I felt an instant connection to this unique girl when we started walking home from school together. I didn't know it then, but my friendship with Paeok during the spring of 1976 would lead to an event that affected me for the rest of my life.

Paeok was adopted at the age of five, along with her three older sisters, by a couple who had been professional ballroom dancers. Paeok's house seemed as strange and chaotic as mine. Her parents seemed too old to be her mom and dad. Ivan was unpredictable. He often sat in his chair, reading the newspaper, and ignoring us completely. But sometimes when he had a beef with Paeok he'd scream at her to get out of the room and out of his sight. I felt sorry for him, but he usually left us alone and he never yelled at me.

The walls of the house were covered with black-and-white photos of her parents ballroom dancing. They were young and dressed elegantly, as if they came straight out of Hollywood. They must have been incredible in their prime. What a contrast to the old man sitting in his pajamas in the living room.

Fawn wasn't anything like my other friends' moms. She must've been sixty-five or older. Her hair and skin were white, but you could still see her pretty face like in the photos. She often wore an Asian robe and kept up with Korean traditions for Paeok and her sisters.

They played Korean music and kept Korean dolls displayed in a hutch, as well as Paeok's Korean dress she wore the day she first came to America. Fawn cooked Korean food, like kimchi and bibimbap. One of Paeok favorite snacks was Fawn's pickled onions. She'd sit us down and scoop out bowls of onions from a large mason jar. I never dreamed of eating onions raw like that, but they sure were good.

Paeok also ate raw eggs! One afternoon, I watched her tap a small hole at the top of one, suck out the egg, and swallow it whole, like how someone would take a shot of tequila. I giggled and squirmed, but Paeok didn't care if I found it funny. For her, eating raw eggs was second nature. In Korea, she and her family had lived in extreme poverty. They had little food and no resources to cook, so she got used to eating raw eggs and learned to like them.

I knew there were poor people in the world, but I never realized Paeok had come from such a desperate place. As I looked at her, I felt a new sense of respect for my friend. Some kids at school made fun of Paeok because she looked different. I never understood where that came from, and it made me angry. I was young and stupid like any other kid, but I knew better than to make fun of people because they were different. I could thank Dad for that. He never put up with intolerance or any talk of bigotry. I'll never forget the day Steve said the N-word in the living room. Dad practically flipped his lid.

"Don't you ever use that word again."

Paeok was the first person I knew who was born in another country. Her family lived close to the war zone in Seoul during the Korean War. She learned perfect English once she came to America, and I was proud to know her.

Paeok's sister Robin still lived at home. She was five years older and knockout gorgeous, with perfect brown eyes and long, golden-brown hair down her back. She had a loud commanding voice, and a big broad smile that reminded me of singer Carly Simon.

Robin was usually home when I came over, lounging around the back den in her silky robes and bamboo flip flops with perfect eye-makeup. She listened to The Beatles and smoked pot with her hippie friends. It was normal to see bongs and pipes and bags of weed spread out on the table. The smell of pot wafted through the house and all the way to the kitchen. When their dad smelled its pungent odor, he thought it was the girls over-doing it with their perfume.

"Stop it with that goddamn spray."

Their mom knew about the pot but didn't care.

Robin and her friends made us laugh because they sounded so stoned and stupid. They didn't offer us any, but one day, Paeok got hold of some, and I smoked for the first time. I didn't like it too much because it made me nervous and self-conscious.

Paeok and I often went to the park to throw a frisbee and meet people, including Robin's friends. One guy, a nineteen-year-old Mexican named Danny, rode a Kawasaki 500 and smoked Pall Malls. He hissed the smoke through his teeth as he inhaled, then squinted his eyes as it floated out of his mouth and nose. I hated cigarettes, and the way he smoked them made it more gross. But Danny turned out to be pretty likable, especially when he told us old Mexican jokes and laughed his head off. Sometimes he would walk with us to the convenient store and buy us sodas and candy bars and became a regular friend of mine.

Still, no one thought it strange that a twelve-year-old girl and a nineteen-year-old man were friends. He even met Dad and swam in our pool a couple times. Danny was never anything more than a friend. When I was young, my relationships with older people were always platonic. Nothing creepy or inappropriate… I was lucky. Something terrible could have happened. My dad never objected to me spending time with Danny. If I had ever explained this to one of my friend's parents, they would have been shocked and concerned. I would have felt embarrassed and humiliated by what my father allowed. How could Dad be so naive?

Paeok and I liked to hang out with Danny at another Mexican guy's apartment, drinking soda pop or beer and listening to music. His name was Tink, short for his last name, Tinkerton. He lived on Hollywood Way about three blocks from my house. Tink was heavy set, over six feet tall and was forty-five years old. He had long dark hair, mahogany brown skin, and enormously big hands with long fat fingers. Sometimes, he played Creedence Clearwater Revival songs on his guitar, which he did extremely well for a man with such big fingers. I brought my Gibson guitar over and he showed me some chords. Dad had bought me the Gibson after he destroyed my first one.

Danny let me ride his Kawasaki 500 in the alley behind Tink's apartment. Dad no longer rode a Harley, but all three of his kids loved motorcycles. It was in our blood. After all, Mom fell in love with Dad partly because he rode a Harley Davidson. My brother had his own Kawasaki road bike and a Husqvarna dirt bike. Allison rode a 400 Honda Hawk that Dad had bought her. I was too young for a motorcycle license, but I rode many different bikes off-road.

It didn't take long to get pretty good on Danny's bike. In fact, I got so good, Danny let me ride around town. But the Kawasaki was way too big for me. The tips of my toes barely reached the ground. We must have been the stupidest people in the world. All of us.

One night, Paeok got on the back of the Kawasaki with me so I could give her a ride home. I always took side streets to avoid the police. When I stopped at the corner of Jeffries and Hollywood Way, waiting for the light, Paeok's weight threw me off and the bike started leaning. When it got too heavy, I told Paeok to jump off and help me push the motorcycle back up. I knew if the bike went to the ground it would be too heavy to get back up. But gravity had its way, and all we could do was ease it to the ground. I turned off the engine and the bike lay cold and silent at the stop light in the middle of the street.

Paeok stayed with the bike while I ran to get Danny.

"If the cops come, I'm leaving and walking home."

We were lucky. Danny got there before anything bad happened.

17
How Do I Ride This Thing?

Paeok and I did everything together. If the weather was right, we swam. If we felt lazy, we sat inside and watched TV, but Paeok and I were social butterflies. Reading a book or watching TV didn't cut it, and we got bored with each other if we weren't around other people.

We knew lots of neighbors and folks around town just by being outside all the time. We used to go to the Texaco station and talk with the guy who manned the pumps. Or we'd go to The Donut House and watch the ladies make donuts, hoping to strike up a conversation.

During one Memorial Day weekend, after we swam in the pool for a few hours, we decided to see what was going on at Tink's place. I grabbed a sweater and went to tell Dad I was leaving. I found him in the bathroom, swabbing his ear in the mirror, fresh from getting a new diamond stud. His new girlfriend, who I hadn't met, had pierced it for him; she worked in the medical field and knew how to do things like that.

I decided not to tell him about going to Tink's because I wasn't sure if he would object, and I didn't want to give him a chance to say no. It was easy to lie to Dad. For all he knew, I was in the child porn industry and pedophile magazines.

By this time, Danny was living in Tink's spare bedroom. We sat on the couch, listening to Led Zeppelin. Danny lit up a joint.

"This is the last of my weed, but we're about to get more."

As of late, I refused to partake for fear of feeling paranoid. Paeok took a hit and coughed hard. After Danny and Tink took a phone call, Danny called me into the kitchen. I left Paeok high in the living room, listening to "Stairway to Heaven."

"Will you give Tink a ride on my bike to get a bag of weed?"

Danny's wrist was too sore to go and Tink didn't know how to ride. I quickly figured Tink was tall enough to keep us upright if the bike started to tilt when we came to a stop. I also liked it that Danny thought I was a good enough rider to run an errand.

"Sure, I'll do it."

Danny high-fived me with his good wrist, and I felt great. By the time we left, it was nearly dark. I thought that was good because if the Burbank cops saw a scraggly White girl riding around with a large Mexican man behind her they would pull us over in a second.

The Kawasaki had a short in the headlight, which Danny hadn't fixed. When I first took off, I had to tap it with my hand to get it back on, but when we got to Catalina Street the headlight went out completely. Catalina had lots of trees, and the yellow streetlamps were dim. I could see Tink's long hair in the rearview mirror, flapping in the warm spring air. Neither of us wore a helmet.

As we approached a red light, I let up on the throttle. Without any warning, a Chevy El Camino pulled out of an alley right in front of me. I never had time to hit the brake. I felt the impact as the front wheel hit the side of the car. I flew over the handlebars, hit the pavement, and tumbled for several yards. I stopped in a sitting position, totally stunned, with no pain anywhere. I got to my feet quickly as my heart pounded.

I was scared as soon as I realized I'd been in an accident. The first thing I saw was the motorcycle on its side. Tink was about ten feet away on his side with his head next to the curb. His eyes were closed, and he looked like he was sleeping. I thought he may have banged his head. I heard sirens approaching.

"Tink! Tink wake up."

Nothing.

Before I knew it, I was sitting on a gurney in the emergency room of St. Joseph's Hospital, hearing the rhythmic clicking of Dad's heels coming down the hall. I was so scared. Being in a traffic accident was a big deal. I was mostly afraid that Dad would yell at me and look at me with disappointment, or maybe even spank me right there in the ER. He hadn't spanked me in years, but I thought this might trigger that kind of punishment.

Dad was in his dancing clothes. His eyes were alert, his face blank and stiff like a statue. I could tell he wasn't that angry. I think he was relieved that I didn't look too bad. He asked if I was all right. I told him I thought I was, but that I hadn't seen a doctor and the nurse had only taken my vitals and walked out.

"Where are you hurt?"

He looked me up and down. That was Dad. He was going to solve this problem as quickly and painlessly as possible. I showed him the golf ball sized lump on the back of my left arm. He pressed it and flexed my arm at the joint. I rolled up my torn jeans and showed him the long scrape on my knee, oozing with blood.

"Let me see you walk."

I could walk just fine. I was bruised and in a little pain, but I wasn't hurt. I knew it, and Dad did, too.

"Let's go, Tracy."

We walked right out. No paperwork. No bills. No nothing.

I didn't see anyone for days. I didn't want to see Mark or call up Paeok. I wasn't sure if she even knew what had happened. It was just as well. I didn't feel like telling anyone about Tink lying in the street, unconscious. I wasn't in trouble. Dad didn't ground me. In my entire life, he never grounded me for anything. But I tried to stay below everyone's radar because I knew I had done something terribly wrong.

During those days I kept my room impeccably clean and did my chores without prompting. When Dad and I crossed paths, or when we ate an occasional meal together, I felt like he looked at me differently. I'd never seen his eyes squint like that. I felt like I had grown up five years overnight. I couldn't stand not being his little girlie anymore.

I never asked Dad what happened to Tink. I was too ashamed. I wasn't even sure he knew. Steve and Alison didn't have much to say, either. It was as if they didn't know an accident had happened. But they knew. Everyone knew.

When my Uncle Willy and Aunt Rene came over, I felt them look at me weird. *What a bad girl*, they must have been thinking.

"*Tsk, tsk, a motorcycle for God sakes? That child is a menace.*"

That's what I imagined them saying. Dad stuck up for me, though, when they asked about what happened.

"It was just a minor accident. The guy pulled right out in front of her."

I guess it was good that people forgot about what happened to Tink, but I thought about him every day. I was too scared to find out for myself what happened to him or if he was seriously injured. I was afraid he had died. So, even after it was over, it really wasn't over. There was still trouble ahead when it came to Tink and that motorcycle.

18
Guilty?

Summer sucked. One day, I headed for The Great Grill to get some French fries. The owner, Pete, knew Dad and was also a bodybuilder, except Pete was way bigger than Dad in every way. I liked going to Pete's because he was nice and gave me extra-large servings of fries.

Where I went wrong was heading down Pepper Street to get to Burbank Boulevard. A kid named Bobby Parker lived on Pepper. He was fourteen and a grade ahead of me, and also hung out at Tink's. I played basketball with Bobby, and he sometimes invited me over for a snack afterward. His mother was a chain smoker and kept her dentures in a cup on the kitchen counter. She told me about the diet she was on, and five minutes later I watched her dump four teaspoons of sugar on a bowl of Rice Krispies. Bobby didn't make much sense either. He and his cousin used to stop by Tink's and brag about stealing a car or beating up a gas station attendant for giving them the wrong change. Bobby turned out to be bad news. I wondered why I had ever spent time with him.

After everything that had happened, I didn't want to see Bobby, but on the way to Pete's I saw him leaning on the hood of a parked car, smoking a cigarette. I prayed he wouldn't see me, but no such luck. He stopped me on the sidewalk and hissed at me.

"I see you're just fine."

He seemed hostile and angry.

"What do you mean?" I knew he was talking about Tink.

"You killed Tink."

Tink . . . dead? I felt ashamed knowing it might be true. I looked at Bobby, not knowing what to say. I could tell he was checking to see if anyone was watching.

"I gotta go."

I knew something wasn't right, and I needed to get away from Bobby. I took a step to go around him. Then out of the corner of my eye I saw his fist. He cold cocked me in my right eye and rode off, just like that, without another word.

He got me good. The whole side of my face throbbed. I made a beeline for home and felt my eye swelling. Dad was in the kitchen. I tried to look away, but he saw me.

"What happened?"

I didn't want him to see me like this.

"A kid punched me."

"Why'd he do that?"

"The guy's a jerk."

"It's not that bad, but you better get some ice on it."

My eye looked like a ripe plum and was even closing up like a defeated boxer. *Not that bad?* It was awful. Dad hardly flinched. I started to wonder if he knew these were repercussions for killing someone. I even wondered if Dad thought I deserved it. I didn't know and I was too scared to find out. Did he know what happened to Tink? Was Bobby going to go around town telling everyone I killed him?

I grabbed a bag of ice and went to my room. By evening, I had a dark blue shiner. Later, Dad poked his head in to tell me he was going to Uncle Earl's and wanted me to come. He'd been bringing me along to all sorts of places lately, another sign he was keeping me on a shorter leash. I had officially lost his trust.

I didn't want them to see me looking like a pitiful tomboy. I was already humiliated. What would I say? It wasn't just the black eye.

Everyone in the family knew about the motorcycle accident. I didn't want them to look at me like Uncle Willy and Aunt Rene had.

Later when my cousin Darlene asked me what happened to my eye, I told her I was hit by a bat during softball practice. It was plausible. Everyone knew I played softball. That lie would be one of many more to come.

19

A Day in Court and Another Lost Guitar

A few weeks later, a county sheriff knocked at our front door. I prayed he wasn't coming for me, but something told me he was. Not long before, a Burbank policeman had come to our house claiming I was stealing mail out of someone's mailbox a couple blocks over. I had no idea what he was talking about. I never stole mail in my life. But with all my carousing, I think some neighbors had a bad impression of me.

"Mail missing? Must be that Steingold girl."

I guess it was the price you pay for having a bad reputation.

It turned out the sheriff was there to give me and Dad a subpoena to appear at the Burbank City Courthouse. A municipal court judge wanted me in his courtroom. Dad speculated it had to do with the damage to the guy's car I ran into. Dad recognized the plaintiff's name; it was the El Camino guy I had rammed.

Three weeks later, I was sitting next to Dad in a half-empty courtroom. The El Camino guy sat across the aisle a couple rows away.

That night of the accident, he'd gotten out of his car and came at me, yelling.

"Where the hell did you come from?"

To make matters worse, an old man on foot appeared and scowled at me.

"She was driving the motorcycle, and it had no headlight."

The whole exchange was troubling and added to the shock I was feeling. It was almost too much to believe, like it was just a bad dream.

That night, the El Camino guy took a few steps toward his car.

"Look what you did to my car."

He was livid. He demanded to know why I was riding without a headlight. I could only shrug. I could hardly believe there was a witness. If it wasn't for the old man, I wondered if I would have lied about who was driving the motorcycle. With Tink still lying there unconscious that night, the thought had crossed my mind. I knew being the driver was big trouble for me. The shame of it all was overwhelming. It was May 1976, and I was only twelve and a half, and I remember thinking I was a *bad* person.

I watched the El Camino guy walk toward the front of the courtroom. He sat at a table with another man, but I couldn't make out what they were saying. My thoughts were suddenly interrupted when I heard the voice of the judge.

"Tracy, are you in court today?"

My heart sped up double time. Dad tapped my leg and told me to stand up. The judge motioned me to come to the witness stand.

"Come up here and sit down, young lady."

I walked down the aisle and stopped short of the witness chair that was terrifying the living tar out of me.

"Come around here."

The judge waved me along.

"I have some questions I need answered."

He leaned over, held out a Bible and told me to lay my hand on it. I couldn't believe this was happening. I didn't have a clue that I would take the witness stand.

"Do you swear to tell the truth and nothing but the truth, so help you God?"

"I do."

I squared up in my chair, keeping a straight confident posture like Dad had coached all three of us throughout our lives. He hated it when I slouched. I looked at the El Camino guy and found him cold and unfriendly, so I turned back to the judge. He was the one who wanted to have a conversation with me. He looked like someone's father, about the same age as Dad, with bright blue eyes and a calm face. He leaned forward and steepled his fingers together.

"Do you understand what is going on here today?"

"No, Your Honor. Not really."

Dad had instructed me earlier that if I talked with the judge to call him Your Honor, just like they did in the movies.

"Well, you're here to help me figure out who's responsible for the damage to Mr. Chamberlin's car. A 1968 El Camino GX."

I took a deep breath. I knew I was responsible for the damage. I was underage, had no license, and was driving without a headlight in the dark. I had no money. I feared that Dad would have to pay and be mad at me even more.

"Do you think you can answer some questions for me?"

"Yes, Your Honor."

"I understand you were the one driving the motorcycle, a Kawasaki 500 that belongs to one Danny Romero. Is that right?"

"Yes, Your Honor"

"Did your father know you were riding the motorcycle?"

"No."

"So, you never mentioned to him at any time you were riding a motorcycle?"

"I would've been in big trouble if he knew."

"Where did your father believe you were?"

"I told him I was going to my girlfriend's house."

"So, you weren't truthful with him?"

"Well, I went to my friend's house, but we didn't stay there."

I lied. I wanted to save some face with Dad sitting there.

"Did the owner, Danny Romero, give you his permission to drive his motorcycle?"

I already knew what I was going to say to that question. I had talked to Danny about it. He begged me not to tell anyone. He wanted me to say I took the bike on my own. Danny convinced me he would get in a lot of trouble if I told the truth. He said he would probably go to jail. I already felt so terrible about what had happened. I just wanted this all to end.

I took a deep breath and looked toward the empty seats in the courtroom.

"No, he didn't, Your Honor."

I glanced over to the judge and back to the seats.

"My friend needed a ride. I know how to ride, and the keys were just sitting there, so I borrowed it. But I didn't get his permission. I wish I hadn't, Your Honor."

I hated lying. I took an oath and lied to the judge like the lowest life form on the planet.

The judge looked in Dad's direction for a moment and sighed. He scribbled on a paper and proceeded to tell everyone in the courtroom his decision. He said that my father was a single parent, working hard to provide for his family. Because he had no knowledge of me riding the motorcycle, he would not be held responsible, which meant that the El Camino guy could not come after him for damages.

I felt a huge sense of relief. Dad wouldn't have to pay a settlement. The judge said that it was up to *me* to compensate the man for the El Camino's bodywork. But how was I going to pay him? It seemed vague, and I don't remember the dollar amount he wanted. All I knew was, I was now indebted to the El Camino guy, and by the look on his face, he wasn't happy. The only one who came off well was Dad. There was no mention of Tink.

Driving home, I was so furious I was on the verge of tears. I hated just about everyone in the world, and it was hard to contain myself.

When we got home, Dad went into the garage, and I went to my bedroom. I opened up all my windows because it must have been over ninety degrees inside. I started cleaning and organizing my albums. I couldn't stop thinking about the courtroom. Tears streamed. I hated myself for lying to the judge under oath in a court of law. What kind of person does that?

I hated myself even more for what happened to Tink. No matter how much I tried to erase the image from my head, I kept seeing him in the street next to the curb. As I lay on my bed, I heard Dad in the backyard. I wondered if he ever thought of Tink. In the ensuing years, Tink's name was never spoken in my family. I never found out what happened to him. Was Bobby right about him being dead? I had walked by his apartment a couple weeks before the court date and the place was empty. My Gibson guitar was there, but I never saw it again.

That wasn't the last time I saw Bobby, either. Later that summer, while waiting for a bus, a sedan cruised past me with Bobby in the backseat, and he looked right at me. I felt exposed, anxious that he might come back and finish the job he started. When I saw a guy on a chopped Harley approach, I stuck out my thumb to hitch a ride. The biker pulled into the bus lane, and I hopped on. I never considered him a threat, especially in broad daylight, and I wasn't going far. It seemed perfectly harmless, and I enjoyed the warm wind in my hair until a mile up the road we came to another bus stop where Bobby and his cousin Yvonne were waiting to board the same bus I was supposed to be on. As we zipped by them, I breathed a sigh of relief. They were probably planning to kick my ass, but I had escaped.

I'm not sure if I deserved a beating for what happened to Tink. I would have fought back, but Yvonne was older and tough as nails. Thankfully, I never saw her or Bobby again.

Allison always said the accident wasn't my fault, that it was Dad's.

"You should have never been in that situation. Dad's the one who let us run wild. You were twelve years old, for God's sake."

Over the years, I've kicked myself up and down, but ultimately, I know that it *was* Dad's fault. But Danny lent me a motorcycle with no headlight. And Tink hitched a ride from a kid. No matter how you slice it, there was plenty of blame to go around.

20

Bad Parents

Dad began taking me everywhere with him—the grocery store, his shop, breakfast at Dupar's, and vacuum deliveries in Studio City. Maybe he thought keeping a closer eye on me would keep us both out of court. Or maybe he was trying to do what a responsible Dad should—spend some time with his kid.

Either way, it turned out to be nice hanging out, just me and Dad. It was like a reunion between us. With all my feelings about the accident and Tink packed deep inside, all I knew how to do was try to ignore them and move on. It was the only direction I could figure out on my own. Dad seemed incapable of helping me process anything. I hadn't even reached my teen years yet, and I already felt confused by the world.

Riding up front next to Dad in his blue 1964 Ford panel van was the best part. When Steve or Allison went along, I always had to get in back, where there were no windows or seats. There was nothing to hold onto and I rolled around with every turn. It was fun sometimes, but I liked it better up front.

We made a habit of going out every week for dinner and a movie. Dad liked going to Hollywood where we'd eat at Love's and then walk down Hollywood Boulevard to check out all the exotic shops and the weird characters. We caught movies at Mann's Chinese Theatre, where we must have seen every Bruce Lee movie ever made.

They were my favorite. One time, we saw the premiere of *Westworld*
with Yul Brynner.

Dad had his favorite stores—May Company, The Acron, Zody's,
and shops on the Burbank Mall. He seemed to make a habit of striking
up awkward conversations with strangers and embarrassing me. Once,
he decided to slip on a pair of castanets, the clicking instrument he
had just bought. When we reached his van, he saw two people getting
out of their car.

"Do you know the castanets?"

He clicked them with a flamingo posture and serenaded them
with a song. The couple laughed, and looked at him like he was an
alien. I was never so embarrassed in my life. But Dad's love of people
had limits. He thrived in their presence, but he also warned me to
watch out for them, too.

"They will stab you in the back in the wink of an eye."

He also counseled me to never lend money to a friend or relative.

"And if you do, don't ever expect to get your money back. Lending
friends money is a friendship killer."

Dad started to seem more concerned about my safety, too.

"You've got to be careful when you're alone walking down the
street."

He wanted me to keep my head up, alert, and to always look
people in the eye.

"Victims are the ones who don't look confident. You never want
to look like a victim."

He wanted to make sure I didn't let anyone touch me in places
that shouldn't be touched. He never spoke to me about sex or making
babies, but he wanted to make sure that no one took advantage of me.
Maybe he finally realized he shouldn't let his daughter run around
with forty-five-year-old men.

"Don't let anyone touch you in your privates."

My face flushed when he said that. I didn't like talking about
sexual things with Dad.

"I won't, Dad."

That same summer, we started going to Dad's new girlfriend's house. He got serious with the woman who pierced his ear. Joanne Bowles. I remember her last name because Dad dated her for several months. Joanne was a medical assistant who worked for a private practice doctor in North Hollywood. She had a boy, Jerry, three years younger than me, and a sixteen-year-old daughter, Jeanine. We went to Parents Without Partners picnics and potlucks with them and even spent holidays together.

Jerry was a miniature Mark. We horsed around the house and played little boy games, like army men and GI Joe, more than I cared to admit. Jerry was always getting in trouble. He did senseless, stupid things, like write on the dining room wall with a black felt marker, or light his GI Joe on fire in the bathroom, or spray paint the neighbor's house. This behavior must have been a symptom of growing up in a single-parent household. Why else were we both so defective? I think I liked Jerry because he made me feel normal. He acted stupid just like me.

Dad and I slept at Joanne's house a lot on the weekends. On Friday nights, Jerry and I watched *Fright Night*. We cuddled on the couch with a blanket, comforting each other during the scary scenes. We loved being scared together. Dad and Joanne were either in her bedroom or on the patio where she smoked cigarettes.

I liked Joanne more and more as time went on. She took my temperature when I was sick and got me seen by the doctor she worked for when I landed on my elbow playing kickball. She treated Dad well, too. She seemed to always smile when she looked at him. I could tell Dad really liked Joanne.

At some point their relationship got so serious that we started looking for a new house to buy, some place big enough for all of us. We were going to be a family.

Then one day we found out Joanne's daughter was very ill. Jeanine had been feeling weak and lethargic for some time. After a few tests, they learned she had a rare blood disease, a terminal cancer of some kind. We were so horribly sad. Joanne fell apart, and eventually she and Dad fell apart, too. A few months later, we heard that Jeanine had died.

I didn't see Jerry or his mom again, but I felt bad for them. I knew firsthand about the pain of death and didn't like the idea of them experiencing it. It made me mad. I wanted Jeanine to be alive again. We could have been a family.

Years later, Jerry Bowles came by Dad's house to say hi. He was tall, well-spoken and had a big handsome smile. Joanne had passed away recently. He told Dad that he just wanted to thank him for always being nice to him and his mom, and that he would never forget him.

21

Best Camp Ever

The summer I turned thirteen, Dad sent me for ten days to Camp Earl-Anna, a Christian summer camp with the Burbank YMCA. The plan came out of the blue, but I liked the idea of going to camp. I thought Dad figured religion might be good for me. Then again, maybe he just wanted me out of his hair and didn't want to worry about me for a while.

Going to camp was nothing new. When we were younger, Mom and Dad sent all three of us kids away while they went to Hawaii and Mexico. I loved every camp I went to, but Camp Earl- Anna turned out to be my favorite oasis away from home.

This majestic place was nestled in a canyon high up in the Tehachapi Mountains, surrounded by pine trees with a cold-water creek running through it. I had endless time to explore new things, like archery, crafts, and riflery, which is where I learned to shoot. There was a huge pool, horseback riding, and campfires every night. Life was perfect, and I never wanted to leave.

On the last night, most of us cried because the thought of leaving that beautiful place was so painful. I didn't. I waited until the next day when the bus brought me home and I saw Dad waiting for me. It was like a floodgate had opened. I was so sad and dismayed to be home. It didn't make complete sense. I knew I had it pretty good with a nice home and a father who loved me, but a lot of things were confusing back then.

The next year, I came home with a small wooden cross dangling around my neck, which I'd made. I didn't fully understand what wearing it meant, but everyone at camp had one and I liked the way they looked—not just when they were kept in a jewelry box.

Dad didn't see it that way.

"You shouldn't be wearing a cross. You should wear the Star of David. You're Jewish."

I didn't understand. Didn't he send me to a Christian camp? What did he think I would learn there? And what about the Baha'is? I didn't wear the cross for long, but I never considered wearing a Star of David. I knew even less about being Jewish.

22
Don't Shoot!

As time passed, Dad lost focus on me again. Before long, I was all over town, hanging out with different friends. One of them, Pam, had problems with her parents, which would affect me.

I met Pam through Betty May, who I met while exploring the LA sewer system with Mark. Lots of kids roamed around the tunnels that fed into the city river. I was always attracted to adventurous misfits who liked to smoke pot and hang out. Betty was fun and charismatic with plenty of freckles, and she loved smoking cigarettes. Dorothy, a short spunky girl, was witty. She always wore bell bottoms and babysat for her neighbors. There were also a couple of good-natured boys who were old enough to drive and gave us rides around town.

Pam came into the picture one day when she joined us in our little powwow in the park. All of us girls went to Luther Burbank. Pam loved frisbee golf and rock and roll. She turned me on to Fleetwood Mac and Pink Floyd, and we listened to their albums on Pam's stereo when her parents weren't around.

After school one day, Pam's father came into the kitchen to get a beer. He looked old and rickety, even though he was the same age as my dad. He had greasy gray hair, yellow stained teeth, and deep creases in his face. I felt proud to have a dad who looked the way he did.

"It's those goddamn hippies," he yelled to Pam's mother, who was watching TV and eating a box of donuts. I wanted one, but she never offered me any and it would have been rude to ask.

Pam's mother was always eating, and she was as round as a pot belly pig. It always embarrassed Pam, who was rail thin.

It wasn't the first time Pam's dad ranted about hippies. Apparently, he had a run in with them back during the Vietnam war. He said they were on the wrong side of everything. I didn't know what that meant, but he sounded angry.

Pam fought a lot with her parents, mostly because her father was often drunk and picked fights with everybody. When I came over, there was usually some negative exchange.

He snapped open his Coors and looked at Pam.

"If you bring a boy home, he better be clean cut and gentlemen like. No hippies."

I took offense at his generalization. Not all long-haired hippies were bad. I knew enough of them to know that. My stomach started to churn. I didn't like his nasty tone. I wanted to say something to defend the hippies. When I finally spoke, I tried to make it sound like I was kidding around. I didn't want to offend Pam's old man even if I thought he was repugnant.

"Well, my brother has long hair, and he's not that bad."

Pam's dad didn't like me speaking up like that.

"Who asked you?"

The following day, Dad got a call from Pam's mother saying I was no longer welcome.

"Did you talk back to her parents? She called you a smart aleck."

I told Dad there must be some kind of misunderstanding.

"I would never talk back to Pam's parents."

"Well, don't go over there anymore."

I was furious. Was it what I said? I didn't understand what the big deal was, I mean, I was always polite to Pam's parents and never once cursed in front of them. Pam told me her mom didn't like me because of how little parental supervision I had.

"She thinks you run all over town and that your Dad doesn't discipline you. Or some kind of bullshit like that."

That sounded about right, but it still made me mad. Pam and I never considered obeying our parents. We thought we knew better. When parents disrespect their kids, trouble happens.

One weekend, when Pam's parents were gone, she had decided to have a little party at their apartment. There was Pam, me, Betty May, and her boyfriend, Dan. We sat in the living room most of the day drinking beer and smoking pot and cigarettes with the music blaring.

Suddenly, Pam's mom and dad were in the doorway in a haze of smoke. The music stopped. Her mom stood there with her hand on her hip, glaring at us. After a few awkward moments, Pam's dad reappeared with a rifle. He stood in front of us and cocked the bolt back with a loud click. His eyes were wild, and he sounded intoxicated.

"What the hell are you doing in my house?"

I wanted to run but Pam's mother was blocking the front door. I thought I could climb out Pam's bedroom window, but her father was in the way. *Is he going to shoot us? Is this really the way I'm going to die?* My mind was racing.

Dan was as scared as me. He was older, with a thick mustache and long hair. He looked a little like a hoodlum. If Pam's dad was going to shoot anyone, it would probably be him.

Finally, Pam's mother spoke.

"Just let them go, Jim."

He eased the gun down and her mom backed away from the door as we bolted past her.

The next time I saw Pam was in the school cafeteria, and she apologized profusely and asked me not to talk about that day to anyone.

"My parents are so embarrassing."

"It's okay, Pam. Everyone gets embarrassed by their parents. My dad probably embarrasses me every day."

I didn't tell her about how I couldn't stop thinking about her father and his gun and the fear of my life ending in her crummy living room. I liked Pam, but it was time for me to move on to another friend and a new hobby.

23

The Van

If my dad hadn't gone to a PWP bowling night in the winter of 1977, he may have never gotten his brass van. That year, Dad's bowling team had a new woman teammate named Sylvia. She hit a bunch of strikes and spares and wasn't shy about boasting about it either. Dad liked her enthusiasm, and the way she looked. She was a hairdresser who lived in Eagle Rock.

Dad took me with him to her house on occasion, and I couldn't help thinking about how close she was to the plaza, where a serial killer called the Hillside Strangler had recently abducted two teenage girls and raped and strangled them before dumping their bodies on a nearby hillside. The killer was still on the loose. You could see the plaza from Sylvia's house, but I never went. I was afraid of that place.

One time, Dad got to talking to Sylvia's daughter's boyfriend who was selling his custom GMC van, which was painted bright orange and red. Dad didn't like his price, but he stewed about the van over the next week.

"I'm going to buy that van, just you wait and see."

A week later, after enjoying Sylvia's pot roast together, Dad said he liked me coming with him. I think it gave him the sense of family he craved.

"It's good to spend time with your dear ole dad."

When we pulled up to Sylvia's that day, the van was in the driveway.

"You still got it I see."

The guy shrugged, like having the van was somewhat of a drag. Apparently, the boyfriend was short of money because he lost his job at the railroad.

"I'll tell you what, I've got four grand in my pocket that says the van's mine. How does that sound to you?"

I had no idea Dad was carrying that kind of cash and was ready to make an offer.

The boy scratched his chin. Dad's offer was $3,000 less than the guy was asking. I stood there eager to hear his response.

"Sure, why not."

Dad reached out to shake on it.

Once he brought the van home, Dad spent hours detailing it. On the inside, he vacuumed every nook and cranny. He even steam cleaned the carpet and the two mini couches. He worked meticulously, scrubbing the entire interior, including the small refrigerator that he stocked with Cactus Cooler and Diet Coke. I loved Cactus Cooler and Sylvia loved Diet Coke.

Sylvia was a bit eccentric herself. She had a huge, round bed in her sunken master bedroom that was painted purple, and she had mirrors all over the walls and on the ceiling. She used heavy makeup that mimicked the look of Elizabeth Taylor, and she styled up her blond-dyed hair like she lived in the 1960's. In many ways, she was just as vain as Dad.

A couple of months after they started dating, Sylvia got a facelift. I didn't understand why someone would do that to themselves. I thought she was pretty, even with a few wrinkles.

Dad broke it off with Sylvia shortly after her surgery. But he came out of it with a vehicle that became his California fantasy van.

It didn't take long before he decided that a few artistic touches couldn't hurt. Dad enjoyed all kinds of art. It wasn't uncommon to see him stare long and hard at a beautiful painting or at a piece of intricate blown glass. Dad appreciated coins as well. He sometimes sat at the kitchen table with a magnifying glass, looking over his small collection, or the newly released presidential coins.

"The detail of this is amazing."

Silver dollars were the first things he riveted onto the van. Dad especially loved the look of the silver dollar. Some in his collection were made of solid silver, but he never riveted those on the van. He loved how bright and brilliant they looked. No other coin compared. Dad had a stock of them in his bedroom closet that he sometimes gave us for spending money. The coins were fun because they were so out of the ordinary, and they felt heavy in our pockets. I always needed to pull up my pants on the way to the candy store.

I couldn't believe he riveted his hard-earned money onto his van. I watched him attach those first coins. He used a two-by-four as a drilling platform. Dad made it look easy drilling through the face of a silver dollar. He already had a rivet gun along with a huge bag of rivets, which were a perfect way to mount things. They were corrosion resistant and strong. If someone wanted to steal his coins, they'd need a drill to bore out the rivets.

I thought those first silver dollars looked pretty cool. He positioned two on the driver's door and two on the passenger door, perfectly symmetrical. If *different* was what Dad was going for, it was certainly that. Who else rivets money on their automobile? Dad fell in love with the idea and decided the van could use lots more silver dollars, and some other stuff, too.

Dad had called me out front to show me two brass elephants from a shelf in the dining room that were now on the hood of the van.

"What do you think? Do you like the look of them here?"

"They look okay."

The elephants looked like hood ornaments.

A few minutes later, Dad riveted them permanently to the hood of the van. He stood back, proudly staring at them. That was it. He was hooked.

Brass turned out to be Dad's preferred metal. He liked it for its bright appearance. Plus, being a soft alloy, it was a pliable metal. He had little trouble drilling through the figures. Brass also held up to the test of time and maintained its brilliance for years. Similar to the Statue of Liberty, which was made mostly of copper and brass, the sheathing was corrosion resistant. Perfect, since his van was always parked outside.

It seemed like brass figurines were calling out to Dad. He started making regular stops at a brass store in North Hollywood. He came home with swords, bells, molded animal heads, coats of arms, animal figures—anything you could imagine.

By summer's end, he had riveted an assortment of safari animals to the side panels along with hundreds of silver dollars. His vacuum business must have done great that year. Either that, or he'd hit it big in the stock market. My dad loved investing.

When I came home from school, he was usually outside working on the van. He mounted coins in straight lines, row upon row. If he had a system, it was definitely geometrical. He'd make circles of silver dollars around a round metal plaque, like an Indian chief or a mini-ship window, and he clustered coins into triangles. The brass was mounted symmetrically. If he put six animals on one side panel, he put six of something similar on the other side.

I think Dad really wanted to be a professional artist. It fit, too. Artists were notorious for going crazy. It sure seemed like Dad was doing exactly that.

During Dad's Harley Davidson days, everyone called him "Chrome Balls" because he stuck shiny balls made of chrome all over his motorcycle. He got them from old Ford cars at a Detroit wrecking yard. Dad thought they looked cool on his chrome-filled bike, and it was a way to make sure it stood out from all the rest.

Dad had also liked to add his own special touches to paintings in our house. One of his greatest works was a painting of an old Latin village that he and Mom got in Mexico. He stuck little mirrors where windows were painted. The main feature of the painting was a painter painting on a street corner. Dad stuck small pictures of my brother and sister onto the easel. He added glitter to the painting, too, plus fake diamonds and little orange tiles for wheels on a bike.

I helped him with some of his projects, like tiling the walls in our house or landscaping the backyard. But I stayed clear of the van. That was just too weird for me. The whole idea of it was bizarre, and I simply didn't understand the point. Sometimes, I even hated the monstrosity.

As the van grew heavier with all the brass, more and more people stared at us wherever we went. Just driving to the store meant we couldn't escape the unwanted attention. I hated being a spectacle, with everyone wondering who those freaks are inside that crazy van.

Dad, however, loved the attention. It seemed like he knew everyone in Burbank. Bank tellers and waitresses knew him by name. Policeman waved. Bus drivers tipped their hats, and other drivers honked their horns to connect with the van man.

I shouldn't have complained too much, though, because in some ways, Dad and his van added spice to our lives. And if there was anything that made the Steingold family interesting, it had to be Dad and that van.

24

Drop Me Around the Corner

The first day of sophomore year at John Burroughs High School did not begin well. As usual, Dad had to roust me out of bed. "Come on. Get up, it's seven-thirty."

He poked his head through my bedroom doorway for the third time. I finally rolled over. No more procrastinating. It took me three minutes to get dressed, brush my teeth and hair, and get to the kitchen, where Dad had a glass of orange juice and a cold piece of buttered toast waiting for me. He handed me two dollars for lunch, and we headed out the back door.

I swallowed hard when I saw the glistening mass of Dad's van. I hadn't thought this through very well. He was going to give me a ride to school in it. The van.

Other than his old Harley Davidson, Dad never had such a cool ride, at least according to him. He thought it was beautiful, and he wanted to do even more with it, so by the end of summer he had hundreds of silver dollars all over the hood and bordering frame. Chains and bells hung around the chrome bumpers. He went overboard like he did with everything else.

I tried to shrug it off as just another one of Dad's silly projects, but it increasingly bothered me throughout the summer. That day, though, was probably the worst yet because I was afraid of what the new kids at school would think if they saw me in that spectacle on four wheels.

While Dad loaded up vacuums to deliver, I took my spot in the captain's chair to ride shotgun. It was too late to change the arrangement. In the side mirror, I caught a glimpse of Dad's Buick Riviera parked across the street. I could talk him into doing a lot of things. Maybe we could take the Riviera instead.

"You don't want to take the Riviera? You said it needs to be driven more."

"I have deliveries. Then I'm going to the store to help Uncle Willy."

I knew the Riviera was out of the question. Since Dad had gotten the van, the Buick had sat covered in dust on the street for weeks. The van was now his primary mode of transportation. I tried to sit back and forget about it. *Maybe the kids at school won't see me.* This would be just another crazy ride in life Dad was taking me on. I could deal with it.

"Hang on girlies."

Dad still used the pet name he called Allison and me, even though I was officially starting high school. As he backed out of the driveway, the bumps caused the bells attached to the van to ring. As we cruised through the neighborhood, people stopped to stare. At a stoplight, Dad looked at himself in the mirror, fingered his mustache to accentuate the curls, and checked if his sutured down toupee was positioned good and straight on his head.

When we reached Keystone Street I panicked. I could see droves of kids outside of my new school. Dad pulled up to the front before I thought to have him drop me at the corner. He stopped at the main entrance where a crowd had gathered before the bell rang. When I exited the van, everyone seemed to stop what they were doing and stare. As I moved toward the steps, I looked for someone I knew. I desperately needed to see a friendly face, someone to support me in this awkward moment. I didn't see anyone, just blank stares and looks of confusion. I passed two boys who were laughing and pointing at the van.

"What the hell is that?"

I heard Dad pull away, but I didn't turn back. As I walked up the steps, I decided that the next time I get a ride to school I would have my dad drop me around the corner. No ifs, ands or buts. That is the way it will be from now on.

25
Ginger

Around the time I turned fifteen, Dad got serious with another lady friend who was from New York City. Her name was Virginia Bowman, but everyone called her Ginger. They met at the PWP and she waitressed at the Coral Cafe. After they dated for a couple weeks, he took me there one afternoon to eat lunch and introduce me to his new flame.

She had red spruced-up hair that looked done-up in a beauty salon, and she wore big fancy earrings. Her manicured red fingernails matched her lipstick, and she snapped her chewing gum as she served her customers. Dad had eyed Ginger as she moved around the cafe. When she passed us, she brushed her hand on his shoulder, and he reached up to touch hers.

"How you doing, babe?"

Once Dad introduced me, she smiled big, showing her straight white teeth.

"Well, how do you do?"

She held out her hand to shake.

"Lunch with your dad. Fantastic."

I liked the way she talked to me with her Long Island accent. She had soft hands for a working woman, and I could see her cleavage when she leaned over.

Whenever she came over to the house, she sat at the kitchen table, smoking Virginia Slims with a glass of Chablis on the rocks. She wore sleek nylon blouses, stretchy rayon skirts that always looked uncomfortable, but she had the aura of a respectable lady. Ginger seemed like a good match for Dad. She liked driving around in the van with all the attention that entailed.

Like Dad, she'd wave and smile. At home, she watched the sitcoms Dad and I liked. I thought she had a great sense of humor, and I liked spending time with her. She was turning out to be my favorite of all Dad's girlfriends.

Three months later, Dad announced he was marrying Ginger. I couldn't believe it. After all this time he was tying the knot. He told me he was marrying her because she was the first woman he truly loved deep in his heart since my mother.

"She makes me feel good. And she can dance up a storm."

He winked and jumped in the pool. Dad was always trying to downplay his emotions. He told jokes instead.

Steve and Allison were out of the house by then, so Dad having a new wife wouldn't affect them the way it did me. I knew it meant big changes, but I didn't mind. I told him I was glad he was getting married.

"Ginger's a nice lady. It will be fun to have her around."

It had been eight years since Mom died. Dad and I were ready to have a new woman in the house.

Dad put his face in the water and blew bubbles. It was a hot day and he liked to cool off without getting his toupee wet. I never saw him put his head under water. As I watched him, I grew more curious about the wedding and the logistics of having Ginger living with us.

"Where's the wedding going to be?"

"In our very own living room. One of my Bahai friends will do the ceremony. We don't want a big wedding. It will be small and inexpensive."

I waded into the water, thinking about the new arrangement. I felt excited, but fearful.

"What does this mean for me, Dad? I mean, Ginger won't try to be my mother or anything like that, right? You'll still be the boss, right?"

"Ginger's a good woman. Just keep your nose clean and everything will be great."

Famous last words.

26

Incompatible

At first, everything seemed fine between Dad and his new wife. Ginger and I got along and there weren't any problems I could see. They were out a lot of evenings together. Dad wore his silky shirts and Ginger wore her fancy nylon and sequin getups. I was usually out, too, drinking booze with my friends at parties or nearby parks. Dad and Ginger didn't seem too concerned about what I was doing, and I appreciated the freedom.

But one day six months later, I found out something had gone terribly wrong. Dad had seemed a bit moody lately and Ginger wasn't nearly as chipper. As it turned out, Ginger was a bigger drinker than Dad knew, and she was often drinking wine before noon. Dad found other things he didn't like. I was oblivious. It wasn't until Dad called me into the kitchen one evening that I got scared about everything.

Ginger was stone faced, smoking a cigarette. Dad was flaming mad about something. He picked up a half-empty bottle of vodka and gave me a grave look.

"We found this under your bed."

I looked at the familiar bottle then over at Ginger, who was blowing smoke deliberately up into the air with her neck cocked back. I looked back to Dad.

"That's not mine. Maybe it's Allison's."

"It's not Allison's. Don't lie to me."

It was true. I was lying. It was my bottle of vodka. I rolled with lots of kids from school who were hitting the harder stuff, and I'd recently discovered that vodka screwdrivers were tasty and easy to make. My friends and I had gotten a bottle for a house party, and when some ended up left over, I brought the bottle home and hid it under my bed. Since Dad was scaring me, I didn't have the nerve to tell him it was mine. When Allison moved out, she could have left it, so that seemed plausible. I decided to continue with the lie.

"I don't drink that kind of stuff. What were you doing under my bed anyway?"

I saw veins pop up on the side of Dad's head. I couldn't understand what was making him so angry. He had never concerned himself with what I was drinking. Meanwhile, Ginger sat quietly, her expression calm and collected, seemingly pleased with what was going on. She had always been nice to me, but now she seemed to be pushing Dad's buttons, making him into a furious lunatic, and he was taking it out on me.

"You better tell me the truth right now . . . or so help me."

He turned away slightly and seemed to glimpse Ginger out of the corner of his eye. Then he hit me in the mouth with the backside of his hand, catching me completely by surprise. I felt the rings on his fingers clash with my teeth. It felt like something broke in my mouth. (Later, Dad told me he saw my teeth fly across the kitchen.) I tried not to cry and hightailed it out of there with the taste of blood in my mouth.

As soon as I left, tears flowed. I went straight to my bedroom mirror and saw two of my bottom teeth were broken. I couldn't believe it. My very own father had hit me in the mouth and broke my teeth. Dad had never hit any of us in the face before. A few years before, he went through a bout of spanking Allison when he was mad at her. She was a teenager at the time. I used to cry when I heard the blows coming from the living room and Allison screaming. But now it was me and I was livid.

When Dad came into the room a few minutes later, I was still shaking.

"I don't know what got into me."

I saw him eyeing my mouth. It looked like tears were building up in his eyes. He looked so sad and miserable and full of anxiety. I almost felt sorry for him.

"You broke my teeth, Dad."

I was still trying to hold back my tears.

"Let me see."

He pulled my bottom lip down and eyed his handiwork.

"Shit. They're broken."

He shook his head and said something so typical.

"They're not too bad. Most of the two teeth are still there. Just the tops broke off."

That was Dad's way of telling me I wouldn't need to go to the dentist.

For the next couple weeks, Dad treated me like royalty. He brought me new socks and underwear. He brought me food from delis and struck up obscure conversations about what he read in the newspaper. He started asking me to spot him when he did bench presses. Dad never asked for a spotter. We talked more than before, but we didn't talk about Ginger.

When I got home from school one day, Allison was stacking boxes on the porch.

What's going on?"

"Ginger's gone. Dad can't put up with her shit anymore."

I saw Ginger's shoes in the boxes, her dresses draped over the porch railing. Everything Ginger had at our house was piling up on the tiled porch.

"She's gone? Just like that?"

"She drinks wine in the morning for God's sake. She's a drunk, Tracy. Haven't you noticed?"

I shrugged. I really hadn't noticed. When she talked to me, she never slurred her words or staggered or showed any other signs of a person who was drunk. Ginger seemed perfectly normal.

"Where is she?"

"Hell, if I know. She's coming to get her stuff. Dad doesn't want her in the house again. He's getting an annulment."

Dad hadn't mentioned any of this. Things had seemed awkward between them, but I had no idea it was this extreme. I learned that an annulment meant it was like they had never been married. I felt heartbroken. I really liked Ginger and enjoyed having her around. Other than getting hit in the mouth, I liked the way things were. I wanted them to make up.

When Ginger came to get her things, I went outside to talk to her. She was about to walk to her car with a load of her dresses on hangers.

"There's no way you and Dad can make up?"

I didn't know why I wanted her to stay so bad. It wasn't like we were exceptionally close and spent a lot of time together. All I knew was she made a refreshing addition to the house and seemed to make Dad happy. Life was more grounded and normal with Ginger around.

She leaned against the railing.

"No, that's not going to happen, Hun. Your Dad and I are what I would call incompatible. For that I am truly sorry."

I knew by the way she spoke that Dad and Ginger were never getting back together. She talked about moving into a friend's house and her daughter visiting from Long Island.

"Stop by the Coral Cafe and see me sometime. You can have a piece of pie on me."

I nodded. I knew that seeing Ginger at the cafe was highly unlikely. I also knew I would probably never see her again. I watched her tearfully drive off. It was just me and Dad again.

This is my brother with some of his buddies in the early days. Kids
from all over town liked to come to the Steingold house.

Happier times were to
come after Mom died.
It just took a long while.
This was right before
things really got crazy.
1973

Age eleven. Life was already getting wild when this was taken. Notice the scar on my left hand. I got that playing around with a knife behind the counter at the Great Grill. 1974

In 1978 my dad met Ginger and finally got married. It didn't last long. I was sad when she left because I really liked her.

The four of us at the house after Dad and Ginger's wedding. We look like we are in shell shock. 1979

Here is Paeok. She was a loyal, true friend and appreciated my dad's brass van far before I did. 1980

The Van before Dad really got started. This is our front driveway where it was always parked. 1979

27

Guilt Trip

Dad still felt guilty about hitting me in the mouth. If I mentioned that I wanted a new basketball, he'd come home with a new one.

"It's made of leather like they use in the NBA."

I got a new catcher's glove for softball and my favorite pair of Vans. When I asked for money to go to the movies, he handed me ten bucks, far more than needed.

"Here you go girlies."

I accepted Dad's gifts like I deserved them, and I was always eager to find out what I might get next. After another one of my bicycles was stolen, we looked for a new one. I loved it when we shopped together. He always courted me for my opinion on things to see what I liked.

"Do you think this lamp would look good in the living room?"

"Do you want a full-length mirror for your bedroom?"

"How about a push button phone instead of that rotary?"

That day, I went straight for a three-wheeled bike in the sporting section. It had two recumbent seats side by side and two pairs of pedals. The price tag said two hundred, thirty-nine. I thought that would be too much, but I waved Dad over to have a look.

"This one would be great."

I thought there was no way he would buy me something so expensive.

The bike had a triangular steering wheel and a carrying basket. He grasped the handlebar, lifted the front end up, and bounced it on the floor. He caressed the seats and checked the sturdiness of the pedals. He looked at the price tag and thought for a few seconds.

"Why not?"

I couldn't believe it. I felt like the luckiest kid on Earth. The bike seemed one-of-a-kind. No one else in Burbank had one. I was sure of it. I had the greatest dad. I went everywhere on that three-wheeler. It was great fun riding around town with a friend in the other seat.

For the first couple weeks, Julie Simmons hung out with me a lot. She slept over sometimes, too. If Dad wasn't with a girlfriend, he made dinner for me and Julie, like soup and a sandwich, or he would offer to heat up TV dinners. We slept in the living room after watching TV, and in the morning we took off on the three-wheeler to explore.

One day we were riding up and down some ramps outside a commercial building. When I pulled the handlebar right and Julie pulled left, we slammed into a pole, leaving a gaping crack between the front wheel and the main frame. I barely got the bike home. When we pulled into our driveway, Julie noticed Dad.

"I think I better go home. He's gonna be madder than shit. The bike was brand new."

I thought it could be repaired since Dad was so good at fixing things.

"Dad, could you have a look?"

"What the hell happened?"

He ran his finger along the crevice in the frame.

"Me and Julie accidentally hit a pole, and it cracked. Can you weld it or something?"

"I don't weld Tracy."

He grabbed the handlebar and lifted the front end, which snapped right off, leaving my beautiful three-wheeler in two pieces.

"Might as well take it to the junkyard because that's exactly what that bike is now. Junk."

He glared at me and walked away disgusted. I brought the broken bike around to the side of the house and left it there out of sight.

A month later, I noticed Stacy, an older neighbor, riding a little Yamaha motorcycle up and down our street with a for-sale sign tacked to the fender. It was a 90cc Enduro with knobby tires and painted bright yellow. I wanted it. Stacy smiled as he passed. When he stopped and shut off the motorcycle, he must have seen the envy in my eyes.

"You want to take it for a spin?"

I jumped up, trying to hide my excitement.

"How much do you want for it?" I asked as nonchalantly as I could. If I had a chance to get Dad to buy me a motorcycle, we would have to settle on a good price.

"I want seventy-five, but I'll consider any offer. Give it a try. I know you can ride."

I hadn't ridden a motorcycle since the night I crashed the Kawasaki. I had been longing to, and I was shaking with excitement. The Yamaha started on the first kick-start. After a couple laps around the block, I wanted that little bike more than anything.

Later that day, I stood near Dad's workbench, thinking of the best way to ask him to buy me the motorcycle. I was nervous and shuffled my feet as I formulated my words. I didn't think it would come down to the money. Dad had plenty and didn't expect me to get a job and make my own. Not yet at least. My real worry was Dad saying something about me crashing the Kawasaki and forbid me from riding again. Since the accident, that question never came up, but I had no idea how he would react.

"Hey Dad. Stacy up the street is selling a little Yamaha 90. It would be really fun to ride up at Indian Dunes. I think he will take fifty bucks for it. Could we buy it?"

The suggestion of riding at Indian Dunes in Valencia was perfect. Riding off-road sounded much safer than street riding.

Dad kept his eyes on the Eureka in front of him.

"Does it run good?"

I felt relieved. He didn't mention the three-wheeler or the Kawasaki.

"It purrs like a kitten. He wants seventy-five, but I think I can get him down to fifty."

"Where would you park it? There's no room in the garage."

"I could keep it in the corner by the fence and cover it with a tarp when it rains."

Dad pulled a fifty-dollar bill out of a box and handed it to me.

"Just be careful. All we need is another accident."

A few minutes later, I had my own little motorcycle. I was ecstatic.

The off-road idea didn't last long. I rode around the neighborhood streets and on some abandoned railroad tracks where no one was around, like the police. I got the best feeling riding that bike, catching the wind in my hair, and watching the neighbors shake their heads.

I always felt like I was getting away with something on that bike. We hadn't learned a thing from what happened with Tink and the Kawasaki. The little motorbike had no taillight and a broken headlight. Imagine the irony. Dad and I certainly didn't. He probably still felt guilty for hitting me, and I was making the most of it.

28

A Nose Like Barbra

During ninth grade, life was full of thriving friendships and positive experiences in my neighborhood and at school. I wasn't academic minded at all, but I enjoyed the bustle. I was open to learning and making new friends.

On my first day of art class, I sat next to the most fun and interesting girl I knew—Tracy Sammons. We had a blast working on art projects. She seemed to know a lot of things I didn't. She grew up in Montana, lived in Seattle, and traveled around Canada. She talked about kissing boys and going to rock concerts. She told me about how people in Montana ate bull testicles and called them Rocky Mountain oysters.

"They're damn right tasty."

She impersonated an old redneck which made me giggle.

Tracy was one grade behind me and one year older. She lived with her single father not far from my house. She had been held back in school when she lived with her mother, who Tracy confessed was a raging alcoholic and wouldn't help her with anything. Tracy had to cook for herself and do all the grocery shopping.

"All that woman did was drink and cater to her fucking boyfriend."

I felt sorry for her having a mother like that. I thought it was better to have no mother at all than the one Tracy described.

Her father, Jim Sammons, moved her to live with him in Burbank, where he was the city's fire battalion chief. Tracy was proud of her dad. She bragged about him all the time.

I met him one day after school. He was in the kitchen drinking a Coors and eating cookies. I instantly felt at home. He was tall and handsome, but he had deep scars on his face that reminded me of the surface of the moon.

Everyone liked Tracy's dad. He had a big speed boat and went deep-sea fishing. He taught me how to water ski and he let Tracy live in his big camper, so we could do practically anything we wanted.

A year later, when I was sixteen, he let me drive his truck and camper on a camping trip to the Chilao campground in Angeles Crest Forest. I think Tracy's dad liked me because he thought she wouldn't get in trouble with me. He thought I was the responsible type and kind of a goody two shoes. I'm not sure what gave him that idea. I think I bonded with Tracy partly because she lived through single-parent syndrome like me. Both our fathers were clueless.

Tracy loved drinking and going to parties. It was crazy how young we were and how much booze we drank. All my friends did. But I got drunk with Tracy more than any other friend I had ever had.

In Burbank, news of a party was quickly passed around school. Sometimes we heard about a gathering at a local park. There was always somewhere to go on a Friday night.

We usually got ready at Tracy's. She lent me her pretty outfits and coached me on how to apply mascara and eyeliner, which I'd never worn. I think she was trying to turn me into a lady. We'd stand at the mirror in her bathroom, Tracy brushing her eyelashes with a mascara stick and me buffing my nose.

"The guys are gonna be flocking to us."

Tracy liked to meet cute boys. She figured if we both looked pretty, there was a better chance of meeting good-looking ones. I was totally onboard. In my post-pubescence, I was constantly daydreaming about kissing a boy and I longed for that kind of attention. But I was far more of a prude than Tracy. She would likely go all the way with the right boy if the opportunity arose. I had fantasies about making out, maybe even going to second base, but having sex was off the table. With the two boyfriends I had in my young life, first base was it, and sex wasn't generally expected in my circles.

Tracy and I were average looking girls, but I was too much on the gruff side for most of the boys I found attractive. I liked the idea of going out with a first-string football player. They had confidence and were often good looking. But those boys had no interest. They saw me as a friend and would rather play football with me and crack dirty jokes, like I was one of them.

I had a pretty big nose, too, which seemed to turn off the boys. Sometimes, I thought of myself as a Barbra Streisand, who had a unique and impressive nose. I thought she was attractive and interesting looking, and her nose enhanced her beauty. I used to dream about pulling that off like she did, minus the singing, of course. My nose had more of a hook to it, though, and I didn't have her confidence. I shuddered at my profile.

It didn't help that Dad often reminded me of my nose.

"It's not the size of your nose that's important. It's what's in it that matters."

Dad thought his teasing was funny, but it mostly made me feel bad.

Sometimes, when I was getting dressed to go out, trying to look pretty, he'd say too much, even though he was trying to compliment my outfit.

"And that big Steingold nose of yours makes it all the better."

Dad took pride in his Jewish nose and thought it gave us character. He was probably right, but I was incapable of grasping that idea. I wanted to be pretty. Getting a nose job would have been nice. I had a school friend who had gotten one when she turned sixteen, and for her it was either rhinoplasty or a new Chevy Camaro. She chose a nose job. I thought she was crazy. Her nose was thin and pointy. It didn't compare to mine.

Going through with a nose job seemed too drastic and vain. I never considered asking Dad, and he never would have paid for such a thing. If I had been given the choice of a new nose or a new car, I would have chosen the wheels.

Cosmetics helped a little. I discovered eye-makeup could draw attention to my eyes and away from my nose. My eyes were my best feature anyway. I also learned to contour my nose with a shadow of bronzer on the bridge, contrasted with a lighter face powder. Dark versus light tricked the eye away from a big protruding honker. My nose needed lots of tricking.

My Barbra Streisand philosophy was the best way to deal with my dilemma. If she could be pretty with her big Jewish nose, I believed I could, too.

29

As If One Crash Wasn't Enough

One February night, Tracy and I met up with a bunch of friends at a park next to the Pierce Brothers Cemetery, where you could watch airplanes takeoff and land at the Burbank airport. Pink Floyd was blasting out of a boombox. We sat on picnic benches under a canopy, drinking Michelob and a bottle of Bacardi. Tracy loved making cocktails even if we didn't have ice.

When the rain stopped, we moved into the cemetery. There was an eerie cold feeling there that always attracted us. This cemetery had a huge domed mausoleum you could walk through, which was especially intriguing to me because Dad had told me a scary bedtime story about the dome when I was a child. He said a large jet had crashed into the dome, knocking it clear off and killing dozens of people. Fires burned while emergency trucks rushed in to help. I gasped at the horror of Dad's story, imagining the poor dead passengers strewn about the cemetery. I also wondered how they got the dome back up. The real story was different. In 1969, a single-engine plane crashed there, killing two people, and severely damaging the dome. I had believed Dad's version for years.

We walked through the eerie mausoleum, imagining all the lost souls as we consumed a lot of Bacardi and Coke. When it came time to leave, we piled into the back of a guy's panel truck where we sat on the carpeted floor. I heard the engine fire up, and we lurched against each other as the truck lunged forward. Two seconds later, we were thrown the other way and came to a sudden stop. The driver had crashed into a parked car. Both vehicles were wrecked, and the front end of the panel truck was steaming in the cold, damp night.

It was well past curfew, and we were all intoxicated. We didn't want anything to do with the Burbank police, so Tracy and I walked toward her house, two miles away. She said the truck engine was in flames and that she thought I was still inside, about to burn to death.

"I tried to put the fire out with my jacket."

"There was no fire, Tracy."

"I was so scared you were still in the truck."

I thought she bumped her head because she wasn't making any sense. There was no fire.

The rain picked up as we walked. I stopped us under a streetlamp to have a look at her because she was still going on about a fire.

"Are you okay? You sound confused."

"I'm fine."

She stumbled and wouldn't look at me. I was positive it was the alcohol talking. Tracy couldn't handle liquor. When she got drunk, she could become belligerent and even hysterical. She didn't remember anything the next day.

One time at a pool party with a bunch of nice, older guys at a condominium in the Hollywood Hills, we swam, enjoyed the jacuzzi, and drank lots of booze. Tracy became extremely drunk, more than I had ever seen. When we got a ride home, Tracy went ballistic. She yelled and said strange things in gibberish that made her sound like she was hallucinating. She scared everyone, and the guy driving decided it would be best to take Tracy to the emergency room. All his friends agreed.

I couldn't believe it. She hadn't taken drugs, and she wasn't in danger. I tried to explain to them that it was just the alcohol, and that she just needed to go home and sleep it off, but they wouldn't listen.

When we pulled up to the ER, I pleaded with Tracy to pull herself together.

"We're at the hospital, Tracy. They're going to put you in a straitjacket if you don't get your shit together."

I was sleeping over at her house that night. How would I explain to her dad that Tracy was in the hospital? He didn't know we drank like we did. He might blame me for not being more responsible. Maybe he'd ban me from seeing Tracy like Pam's parents had done with Pam.

When a nurse and orderly came out with a stretcher, the nurse looked at Tracy talking to the ceiling of the car.

"It looks like PCP."

That almost made me laugh. The nurse was so wrong. When Tracy heard that, she looked at the nurse wide eyed and became coherent.

"I'm fine. Please just take us home."

I felt like we had just dodged a bullet. Tracy slept it off in her camper and everything was fine by morning.

Now Tracy was just as delirious.

"I smothered the flames with my jacket."

By the time we got to her house, I was so pissed I wanted to go home. It must have been three in the morning, but I decided to take everything I had at her house and never come back. This included my Yamaha XL90. Tracy and I had been riding it around in a vacant lot next to her house.

I was only seven blocks from home and no longer buzzed from drinking. I put on the three coats that I'd accumulated at Tracy's house, threw on my backpack, and took off in the dark of night. My plan was to get home without being seen. Everything was going well until I saw headlights coming. I thought I'd better pull over and let the car pass because if it was a cop I would probably go to jail. Second, I had no headlight, and cars can't see you if you don't. The street was still wet, so when I hit the brakes, my rear wheel skidded, and the force threw me off the bike. I tumbled over and smacked my elbows and right knee on the pavement. I sat up and watched the car I was avoiding pass by.

My coats must have saved my arms because they didn't hurt at all. But when I stood, my right knee buckled with considerable pain.

"Shit. I broke my leg."

I tried to put weight on it and seemed okay, so as I limped toward the motorcycle my leg buckled again; it was scary to feel something moving inside it. I needed to get home, so I took more deep breaths and limped as straight as possible heel to toe, hoping my leg wouldn't buckle again. I made it to the motorbike, picked it up, and managed to walk slowly home.

Once inside, I crawled to my bedroom and took off my shoes and socks. I didn't have a bra to worry about since I was still flat as a pancake. All I had to do was take off my pants and crawl into bed. Once I was in position, I realized I hadn't closed my bedroom door, and I could hear Dad snoring down the hall. I knew I hurt my leg badly. The thought of telling Dad scared me more than anything since my last accident.

Early the next morning, I called Veronica, my true and warmhearted friend, who lived across the street. Since her recent divorce, I'd spent more time with her and her two young daughters. Unlike most women in my life, who made me feel uncomfortable by telling me how I should dress or do my hair, Veronica was easy to be around. We talked about the Dodgers and Rod Stewart. She even grew marijuana in her yard because she thought it looked pretty and that she might smoke it one day.

"Let's see if it makes flowers."

She had to be the coolest adult I knew.

Veronica made the best tacos and called herself my pretend mom.

I was convinced that getting hurt on a motorcycle again was going to make Dad go ballistic, and I thought having Veronica at my side could deflect his anger.

Dad knew Veronica. Sometimes, she brought him a plate of her homemade Mexican food. They sat out by the pool eating lunch and drinking beers, rambling on about nightclubs or the best restaurants. I was amazed how they could talk so endlessly. They seemed so different, but I thought Dad considered Veronica not just a neighbor, but a friend.

Sometimes, I imagined them as a couple. I would have taken her as a stepmom any day. But Dad was too old and eccentric for Veronica. There was no way she would go for him.

Veronica answered the first ring. Her calm, cool voice soothed me immediately.

"What's going on? Tell me what happened."

I told her the whole story, sparing no details about the drinking and Tracy and the crash.

"You were able to walk the motorcycle home, so maybe it's not as bad as you think." She assured me that Dad wouldn't go ballistic and that she would come over later to be there when I told Dad. But Veronica got a call from her boss, and since she didn't want to leave me in the lurch, she called Dad and told him what had happened. I was sound asleep when he came into my room. Veronica must have spoken some magical, motherly words to him because when he asked me what was wrong with my leg he seemed calm and reasonable.

As usual, Dad performed his own physical assessment. His Army medic days were still a part of him. He took a good look at both knees. There were no scrapes or visible bruising, but it was a little swollen. He told me to stand and walk. I paced back and forth, and my knee didn't buckle but it still hurt, and I had a pretty big limp. But in those days, we figured that if you can walk then nothing must be broken.

"I think you'll be alright."

I wanted to believe him.

I kept limping for the next week. I tried to believe I wasn't badly hurt but my leg didn't feel any better. After two weeks of agony, Dad finally took me to a doctor who said it was just a bad sprain. Wrap it in an Ace bandage and ice it for the next few days.

The doctor's reassurance must have had a placebo effect because I started doing more things even though my knee still hurt.

As for Tracy, I didn't talk to her for weeks after the crash. I realized that her drunken tirade had everything to do with her dad. She loved to brag about her fire chief dad and all the lives he'd saved. I thought

Tracy wanted to save people's lives like him, except she could only save them in her mind, and that got convoluted whenever she drank.

Her dad really was a hero, a trained professional who took charge in hairy situations, something I never expected from my own father. But then again, my dad wasn't a fire chief. He had other magical powers.

30

The Fake Consent Form

I was sitting with friends one day at school when Shelagh pulled out a Young Life consent form for a beach trip with the Christian youth group. Shelagh wasn't religious, but we all got to thinking that a trip to the beach without adult supervision would be more fun.

There was no way our parents would let us go on a camping trip by ourselves, not even my dad. But this was an adventurous group of friends, and we partied a lot together. Chris had a cool idea and Shelagh was on it right away.

"Could we make our own consent form?"

"Yeah. I'm not sure how, but couldn't we make our own forms with whatever information we wanted, like dates and everything, and have our parents sign it? They would never know the difference."

It occurred to me that I could do that in my print shop class. No one had computers or used typewriters much back then, but I had access to a print shop, so I volunteered.

Kelly, who I knew since second grade, had a big conscience and wasn't as enthusiastic.

"You guys realize what you're saying, right? We're going to lie to our parents, have them sign a fake form, and go camping at the beach by ourselves. We don't even drive yet."

Cindie laughed.

"It sounds a little crazy, but we would have a blast."

I was with Cindie the night I was thrown into the back of a Burbank police paddy wagon for a curfew violation. We were standing outside a 7-Eleven with a hundred other kids who had been cruising Burbank Boulevard for fun when the police swarmed in. They put twenty of us into the back of a wagon. Just to be obnoxious, we started rocking it with our weight. The cops kept telling us to stop. It was a great night even though we both ended up at the police department. The amazing part was that Cindie and I didn't get in trouble with our parents.

"I think we should do it."

I agreed with Cindie. I loved the idea.

Kelly pushed the form toward me with a big smile on her face.

"Okay, Steingold. You better make them look good. If my mom finds out, I'll be in the deepest shit that shit can go."

Chris smiled. I knew she would be on board.

I was in an advanced graphic arts class and had been doing print shop since junior high school. I could print just about anything.

In ninth grade, I learned silk screening to print T-shirts. During basketball season, Mark and I put together our own girls' team. Mark coached me and eight of my girlfriends, including Betty, Pam, Dorothy, Chris, and Rita. Even though most of the girls smoked cigarettes and drank beer, we practiced every week and turned out to be fairly good. Dad sponsored our team and bought us plain blue tank-tops, which I took to my graphic arts class and silk-screened *Dreese Vacuum* on the back with a number. We had a blast and advertised Dad's business.

My graphics class learned to print business cards. We used traditional letterpress printing where you assemble the text letter by letter into a composite stick. You place the composed plate into the printing press and feed the machine card by card. Up until the twentieth century everything was done on letterpresses. I decided to make five hundred business cards for Dad, and he used them all.

When it came to the forged consent form, printing them wasn't as easy as I thought. My teacher Mr. Rouse walked the print shop floor that day, paying close attention to everyone. He was one of the nicest teachers. He had long hair and the kind of laid-back attitude that made you think he indulged in reefer every once in a while. But I had no idea what he would do if he knew I was printing bogus consent forms in his class.

I made the changes I wanted to the original form then burned a plate for the offset press. Mr. Rouse liked to make sure everything was running smoothly and that students were being safe. When he was helping someone, I made my move to the one-color offset press. I nervously loaded my plate, turned on the power and made the ink adjustments. I only needed five copies. But every second I spent at the press made me feel paranoid and frantic. What would Mr. Rouse think of my scheme to trick our parents?

Just as I feared, Mr. Rouse showed up when I pulled out my finished prints. Did he read something in my expression or body language to clue him that something unholy was going on?

"What you got there?"

He sounded genuinely curious.

"Not much."

I reached down to remove my plate from the press.

"Just a stupid form I made up for a class."

"Young Life?"

"It's a social studies thing."

I lied as convincingly as I could, but I didn't think I was doing a good job.

"Yeah, right."

Mr. Rouse walked away shaking his head. He had let me off the hook.

31

Ventura Beach

Our beach weekend in April 1979 was a trip I'll never forget. Everything went according to plan. Even Kelly lied to her mom and had her sign the form. My leg was still sore from the motorcycle mishap, but I was determined to go.

Ventura Beach shared a county line with Los Angeles, which meant the sheriffs rarely questioned anybody, not even fifteen-year-old girls sleeping in the sand. There were five of us that weekend—Cindie, Kelly, Shelagh, Chris, and me.

Chris and I were closer than ever, and I considered her my best friend. We connected in gym class in seventh grade when we beat everybody's asses in the strength tests. Chris was as strong as me, and one of my fiercest competitors. When we swam in my pool, we raced, but it was always good natured, and we always enjoyed each other's company.

Whenever Chris came over, she insisted on watching Dad work on his van. She was captivated by how he riveted the ornaments. She asked him questions about the brass and wondered how many silver dollars were attached.

"Count them and let me know."

Chris's parents always welcomed me, and they were almost as lackadaisical as my dad. But as it turned out, Chris's mom cared more than we knew.

On the day of our trip, my brother Steve's girlfriend drove us to the beach in Dad's Riviera. She agreed to give us a ride without us telling her any details of our plan, but when we started unloading our things, Lisa looked at me skeptically.

"Are you guys going to be okay?"

"We'll be alright. Shelagh's older brother is giving us a ride back." That was a lie.

"Just don't say anything to my dad."

"Great!"

She rolled her eyes and left us in a cloud of dust. As we looked for a camping spot, we noticed lots of people on the beach, including guys riding three-wheel ATV's, surfers, and picnickers. We made camp on the Los Angeles side next to some sand dunes and a huge tree trunk that protected us from the wind. We had sleeping bags, a tent, food, lots of beer, and a bottle of Johnny Walker scotch. A shallow river flowed under the bridge, which was nice because the water seemed clean, and I liked that we could wash off the salt water if we wanted. I didn't see a bathroom anywhere.

One of the guys riding an ATV was Chris's friend. When Zachary offered to let us have a turn, I was a little skeptical. I had grown far more cautious about riding, and my knee was still sore. Those three-wheelers also had a bad reputation as being unsafe and were eventually banned from being manufactured in the US. But I had to give it a whirl.

As soon as I saddled in, I knew it was a bad idea. My knee hurt as soon as I hit the first bump and swelled up after that, leaving me limping through the rest of the day.

Before nightfall, we collected driftwood and newspaper and built a campfire. As it got dark, we were the only ones on the beach. We cooked hotdogs and drank some Johnny, which tasted like diesel fuel. Zachary and his friend showed up with three girls from Reseda. The sound of crashing waves and the bright stars above made a perfect atmosphere. It felt liberating, like we could do anything we wanted.

Chris hit Johnny hard and got so drunk that she suddenly decided to head to the water. I followed her because I didn't like her being out in the surf alone. The big waves were dangerous, especially for a drunk person. I followed her along the shoreline until she finally came out, then helped her get back to the fire. Zachary's friend was there, smoking a joint. Everyone else had gone to the store on the highway to use the bathroom. The boy didn't say much or offer us any pot. I thought he was painfully awkward and a complete stoner, but he seemed nice enough.

I had to take a pee, so I found a place behind a log. There was no way I was walking to the highway. It was too far with a bum leg. When I got back to the fire, I spotted the boy's hand down Chris's blouse, massaging her boob. She looked unconscious. As soon as he saw me, he pulled his hand away. I was enraged. *The nerve of this guy!* I walked up and flicked him square in the nose with my finger, like a little kid would flick a cardboard football on a tabletop.

"How dare you."

He tried to grab me, like he wanted to get even, but he missed. I helped Chris up and brought her to the tent to sleep it off. Luckily, that was the end of it. The next morning, my knee was throbbing. I knew there was no way I could stay another day. I had to go home.

The girls from Reseda were hitchhiking back to the valley and said I could go with them. I only hitchhiked a few times in my life because I knew it was risky; I thought it would be safe with three other girls. We caught a ride in an old Chevy Impala to Reseda, where I took a bus to Burbank that dropped me two blocks from my house.

That evening, the telephone rang. It was Jenny, Chris's mom. Had she learned about our ruse? Why else would she call? I wasn't prepared to think up a plausible lie.

"No, she isn't here."

I tried to speak in a higher pitch, but she recognized my voice.

"Is this Tracy?"

"No, this is her sister, Allison."

"Where is Chris?"

"I'm sorry but I have to go. There is someone outside waiting for me."

I hung up, overcome with panic. I imagined Chris's mom knocking on our door. If I hid and didn't answer, would she look through the windows? I locked the doors and closed the drapes. I hadn't seen Dad who didn't know I was back early. If he came home now, when Chris's mom showed up, I'd have to explain the whole bloody plan and confess that Chris was still at the beach. I had to get out of the house. Veronica's house was dark. I saw lights on at Mark's, so I limped across the street and stayed there for the rest of the evening.

Chris came over straight from the beach the following afternoon, looking weathered. I could see a beet red burn on her forehead as big as a silver dollar.

"What happened to your head?"

"It's what you call a flaming marshmallow attack, and the marshmallow won."

I leaned in for a better look. There were small burns on her nose, bubbling with blisters.

"It hurts like hell. I had to stick my face in the ice chest. It was horrible."

Chris sat and let out a deep sigh.

"I'm gonna call my mom to pick me up."

I told Chris how I pretended to be my sister. Chris never had her parents sign the form and had told her parents she was going camping with my dad and me. I thought that was a stupid story because Dad never took me camping. But that explained why her mom called. She picked up Chris and our parents never found out about our trip.

32
My Exploding Knee

On Monday morning, I had Dad drop me off at school around the corner; I'd been having him drop me there all year to avoid any more van humiliation.

My limp was almost nonexistent. I felt so good, I figured playing basketball in PE was possible. It was my last class of the day, and once we got outside, my knee felt fairly strong and hurt only slightly. I was up for a game of two-on-two.

I was able to move around the court okay. At one point, this big kid raised his arms and forced me back with his swift defensive moves. My knee buckled with the most excruciating pain I had ever felt. I fell to the ground, screaming in agony for Mr. Hearst. He knelt, lifted my head, and placed it on his jacket.

"Take some slow deep breaths."

My knee became the size of a football in a matter of minutes. I began to feel nauseous. I was going into shock. Mr. Hearst kept trying to calm me down.

"Take some slow deep breaths."

Kids kept telling me I looked stark white and that my eyes were rolling up in my head.

"I need my dad, Mr. Hearst. Get my dad."

"Okay. Just keep those steady breaths going."

I ended up in his office in a wheelchair, icing my knee until Dad came. Mr. Hearst was a wonderful older gentleman who also coached football and track and field. A year later, he became my shotput coach.

I had three fractures in my right knee. The orthopedist pointed at the X-ray that my first doctor had taken weeks before. Dad and I already knew that he was a quack who obviously couldn't read a fucking X-ray. But there was no use bringing that up.

We were lucky because earlier that year Dad had bought us medical insurance for the first time. My screw up wouldn't be a financial blow because Dad had me lie about how I hurt myself. He didn't think an unlicensed motorcycle riding injury was covered, so we said it was a bicycle crash. I wasn't a good liar, but it was a plausible story, and we just ignored the fact that the bike had an engine.

The doctor drained my knee with a large bore needle attached to a huge syringe. I forced myself to watch for a second as he drew back on the syringe that filled up with a red serous fluid. Then he put me in a full leg cast and gave me crutches. Dad had to go to work and wasn't sure what to do with me. I agreed to go to school instead of missing class.

When Dad pulled up in front of school, Ellen Pierce was waiting for her mother to pick her up for a dentist's appointment. Ellen was a close friend by then, but our first encounter was a fistfight in third grade. She had made me so mad at the jungle gym that I punched her in the stomach; she buckled over in pain. Little did I know that Ellen had bilateral hernia surgery a week earlier and was still fragile. I felt like an awful person. Dad, Ellen's mom, and the principal were upset, but Ellen was fine. I told her I was sorry, and we became great friends.

I wasn't sure how to get up the stairs on crutches, so Ellen came to my aid.

"Are you sure you want to go to class right now?"

Dad was still at the curb, making sure I got inside. I was on the verge of tears, totally unsure why I was going to school. I could have gone home with a good excuse. I saw Dad and the van, and at that moment I didn't care that the van was a stupid circus. I had bigger problems and was glad Dad hadn't left.

"Just a minute, Mr. Steingold!"

Ellen wanted to talk to him, so I went back with her to the van. Ellen knew a lot about being in a cast. A couple years ago, she had broken her ankle when Mark and I brought her to play frisbee and climb the roof of our junior high school. Ellen was afraid to jump, and when she finally did it didn't end well. Ellen didn't come to school for a whole week and ended up in a cast for months.

"Mr. Steingold, it might not be the greatest idea for Tracy to move around so soon after getting that cast on."

Ellen gave me a reassuring look and told Dad that the plaster was still forming.

"You're probably right. Let me take you home, kiddo."

When the cast was removed three weeks later, the orthopedic surgeon recommended a knee arthroscopy. If I had a tear of the meniscus, as he suspected, my knee would have to be surgically repaired.

I was petrified heading into the operating room. I started to cry when they came to wheel me in. Dad was right there.

"You'll be fine girlies. Hang in there, kid."

The great thing about Dad was how much he loved me. I didn't fully realize it until I was a grown up. For a long time, all I saw was Dad being self-centered. But that day in the hospital he didn't leave me alone knowing my problems were being solved. When I awoke after surgery, Dad was reading a magazine. I loved him sitting there. It made me feel important. He stayed through the evening until the doctor came by. My medial meniscus had been damaged, and he had performed something called an arthrotomy to remove it. Underneath the operative dressings, the scar on my knee was four inches long.

The surgeon stuck out his open hand and hovered it above my knee.

"Can you lift your leg off the bed and touch my hand?"

I strained to lift my leg, but it wouldn't budge. My strength seemed to have vanished in the operating room.

"Keep working on it."

I wouldn't be discharged until I could lift my leg off the bed.

The next day, Dad was back and so was the doctor who hovered his hand again over my leg and told me to lift it. I strained and fought with all my might. It still wouldn't budge. While I was in the hospital, I could never lift my leg off the bed. The doctor assured me my knee would make a full recovery, but that it would be susceptible to arthritis when I got older. After four days, I finally went home and began to think I had a dad I could finally count on. Or something like that.

33

Be All I Can Be

The best part of life with Dad was the freedom it provided. If I wasn't lounging around the house watching TV or sunbathing at the pool, I was out, partying with my friends. As long as I stayed out of trouble and kept my room clean, rules and regulations were null and void. I wouldn't call it a life of privilege, but it was easy compared to many other kids I knew. I was lucky, even with everything that happened to me so young. Still, I lacked direction. I never had a job for any length of time, and it seemed like the only worthwhile thing I did in school was sports.

After my knee mended, I joined my high school track-and-field team and threw the shot put in junior and senior years. Mr. Hearst taught me how to heave it glide-style. I was strong, with lots of muscle mass, and I did quite well in competition.

At home, I rarely spent time with Dad. Now that I had my driver's license, I drove his Riviera to school and ran my own errands. Dad was often with his girlfriend at night, or I was out with friends. We barely crossed paths for long stretches. When we did, I told him about my upcoming track meets because I wanted him to watch me throw. After he missed my first two meets, I began to have doubts he'd ever come.

The week I competed against Burbank High, while warming up, I saw Dad leaning against the fence at the edge of the track. I felt my

151

chest rise with warm energy when he waved. I picked up my shot put
and rotated it eagerly in my hand. I loved having him as an audience
member. When it was time for my throw, I broke my personal record.
It was the first meet I had ever won first place. At home, Dad kept
telling me what a great throw it was.

"I didn't know how good you were. Keep up the good work."

Dad rarely encouraged me. So, I was surprised, and it got
me thinking. I couldn't recall ever talking to him about my
accomplishments or what I might do with my life. I don't think stuff
like that crossed his mind. Between his business, girlfriends, and the
van, I was an after-thought.

Playing sports was a good way to spend free time, but I was starting
to feel like time was running out. I was nearing the end of junior year
and was nowhere close to being prepared for life after high school.
That thought haunted me. My brother had become a house painter,
and my sister made a good living waitressing. But I didn't want to do
those things. My grades were average, and I hadn't considered college.
I needed to come up with a plan for the future. I was a good shot-
putter, but I was no Olympian. Too small. I'd seen the women shot
putters on the East German track-and-field team. They looked huge
and unsightly, and I didn't want to become like them, but being in the
Olympics was my ultimate fantasy.

At the beginning of senior year, I had a bunch of friends over for
a pool party. While we were busy in the pool sucking on Michelobs, I
decided to broach the subject.

"So, what's everybody doing after graduation?"

Not all my friends were unmotivated underachievers like me.
Lucy was going to UCLA, Chris to a community college, and Ellen
had chosen a local school to become a dental hygienist. As I listened
and thought about staying home, finding a job, or going to a local
college, I became more and more bewildered. I didn't want to remain
in Burbank or Southern California. I wanted to get away and explore.
I needed a plan.

A mental bell dinged when a fellow student told me she was planning to join the Navy right after graduation. Enlisting was easy; she would be learning a trade and traveling the world. She glowed with excitement.

I had considered enlisting in the military a few months earlier after seeing a recruiting commercial during a football game.

"Get an edge on life in the Army. Be all you can be."

I wasn't buying what they were selling. It sounded like a fairytale, and really like a bunch of grunt work. Still, I liked the sense of teamwork portrayed in the ad. I liked the idea of being a patriot and serving my country and belonging to something that could provide a viable future. Dad had been a military man. *Should I be a military woman?*

But I put the idea on the back burner and never thought about it again. This time, after hearing about the Navy, I decided to look into it further.

I read about the Army, Navy, Air Force and Marines. The Navy won me over. The librarian gave me a booklet, which explained Navy history and the division created during WWII, called the WAVES. Women had a strong history of service in the Navy and that inspired me. I was sentimental like that. It was a four-year commitment, which I thought I could handle.

Learning technical skills, like electronics and computers, could translate into a good civilian job. I could also sail on big ships and see the world, or even become a pilot. I had always dreamed of flying. Most importantly, I could get away from home.

By the time I left the library, thoughts of boot camp and sailing on a destroyer were racing through my head. If I liked it, maybe I could become an officer and make it a career.

When I got home, Dad was working on his van, which now had thousands of pieces on it. The thing looked massive. Dad was proud.

"I'm creating a national monument."

He and his van had gained some notoriety, but a national monument? The attention he got was impressive. He was going to be on a national TV show called *Real People*, as well as in a few local parades. A dozen articles had been written about Dad and his van; he was making a name for himself.

"How was your day?"

"I'm joining the Navy."

I wasn't sure if telling him was a test or a factual declaration.

Dad nodded, tilted his head in thought, and started coating another piece of brass with Future, his polish of choice.

"Why not the Army? I was in the Army."

"I know, but I like the Navy better."

"Yeah, the Navy is a good branch. When did you decide that?"

"About five minutes ago, I think."

"Well, it's a big decision."

It sure was.

The following week, I went to the recruiting office. The first steps included an aptitude test and passing the physical. I was overweight at the time and my recruiter, a chain-smoking fast talker who had not one but two framed pictures of Ronald Reagan on his wall, told me I had to lose fifteen pounds or I might not pass the physical.

For the next four weeks, I dieted the best I could. I didn't eat candy bars or the Ding Dongs and Oreos in our cookie jars. I didn't lose much weight. Someone told me I could lose water weight, so the morning of the physical I swallowed diuretic pills and peed away every ounce I could.

After I finished the two-hour aptitude test, I waited for the physical exam, nervous that I hadn't lost enough weight. Inside the exam room a male doctor listened to my heart and lungs and checked my eyes and throat. The scale said one hundred fifty-eight, which I thought was too much, since the weight limit was based on height. When I stood by the wall to be measured, I stretched my spine while keeping my heels down. I took a deep breath, sucked in my stomach, expanded my shoulders, and held it. The doctor walked behind me and bent to get a closer look at my legs. I was wearing a hospital gown. He seemed skeptical.

"Did you have polio as a child?" He sounded completely serious.

"No." I was indignant.

"Just stand still, flat on your feet."

I didn't pass the physical. I was overweight. Everything else was fine. I had a decent score on my placement test, but apparently the Navy didn't want chubby girls. My recruiter said I had to wait six months to take the physical again. I had my doubts that would happen. I didn't feel like I had time to wait around for the Navy. I was instantly turned off and I told myself that it was their loss.

34

My Big Decision

If I couldn't get into the armed forces, I had to do something. A minimum wage job wouldn't cut it. The only two jobs I'd had were delivering flowers and stocking the shelves at Newberry's during the holidays. I needed training. I could apply at the airport to sell tickets or maybe drive for one of the movie studios, but those occupations didn't appeal to me. I wanted a career. I wanted to specialize in something worthwhile and be a professional. I needed to go to college. Why hadn't I figured this out sooner?

In late October, I decided to see Mr. Kale, my guidance counselor. I told him I wanted to major in something that took place mostly outdoors. I didn't want to be a paper pusher working inside an office. Mr. Kale licked his finger as he shuffled through my transcripts. *GPA 2.2.*

"Well, I wouldn't call your grades stellar."

"I know. But I can still get into college, right?"

He smiled. "I think there must be something for you."

Mr. Kale informed me that I had barely enough credits to graduate, that I couldn't get below a C in any of my classes. I would have to add a seventh class in my last two terms to make up credits. That meant getting to school by seven-thirty every school morning for the rest of the year.

"I can do that."

I nodded to emphasize my determination.

My social studies teacher was giving away ten points of extra credit to anyone who donated blood to the Red Cross. That got me across the finish line, so I essentially gave away my blood to graduate high school.

I made it clear to Mr. Kale that I wanted to get away from the city and the LA smog.

"I get that. When I was a kid, my mom wanted me to live at home while I went to college. There was no way that was going to happen."

He handed me a catalog for College of the Redwoods. "How does forestry sound?"

"You mean like being a forest ranger?"

I instantly loved the idea. It was a job caring for nature. I had always loved spending time in the forest. Camping and backpacking had been my favorite pastimes since I was a kid. Mr. Kale said a degree in forestry could get me all sorts of different jobs, like wildlife and park management, or conservation and botany. Getting paid for working in the forest was a great idea.

The college was in Northern California near the giant Sequoia redwoods. I could go to school far from home in a forest! The tuition would be in-state, and I was likely eligible for a government grant.

My mind was made up. I was going to Eureka, California to go to college. I felt a huge smile spread. I'd never been so excited and motivated about my future, and now I had a viable plan. I wasn't even seventeen, but I wanted to leave home more than anything. Dad and I got along alright, and I still had a lot of freedom, but I was like any other teenager. I wanted to grow up and get away, and college was my ticket.

The shot is a bit blurry, but I can see my dismay. At the age of fourteen, I was on a path to break myself one way or another. After I crashed my motorcycle, my knee and athletic aspirations took a hit. But throwing the shot put and being driven around in a crazy van was still in my future. 1978

Tracy Sammons was the biggest partier I ever knew and a good friend. Her battalion fire chief dad was also a good man and a hero in my eyes.

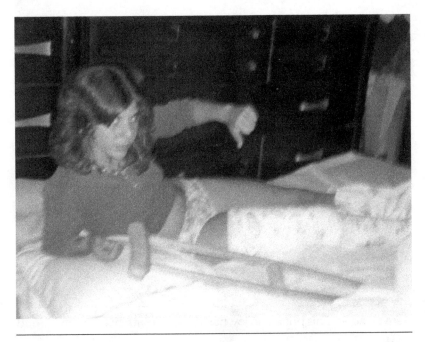

I was not a happy gimpy person. About May 1979

Here's the little motorcycle that was my knee's doom. It was entirely a piece of junk. Let me just say, it was a series of unfortunate events.

Here's Dad and his pride and joy, posing again with his shirt off around 1980.

Pre-high school graduation party, June 1981. Some of these girls were my closest buddies throughout my school years. I must be taking the picture.

From Left to right. Tracy Sammons, Shelagh O'Neil, Cindie Neeley, Tristy De Felicis, Chris Noel, Kelly Walker and Rita Torres.

This picture with my dad and Veronica, my pretend mom, is a true treasure. Deep inside I always knew I would graduate, with pool hair, no makeup, and my bathing suit on underneath my robe. It was in the high 90s that day. June 1981.

We all made it to Dad and Gretchen's wedding. May 1982. Notice I am wearing the same dress when he married Ginger. I weighed probably close to 155 pounds. Too much weight to get into the Navy, I learned. But I got into the dress.

35
Eureka! Here I Come!

Meanwhile, Dad seemed to have met the woman of his dreams at a PWP dance. Her name was Gretchen, a waitress at the International House of Pancakes. She wore fancy jewelry and cowboy boots. She seemed nice, and most important she seemed to adore Dad, and of course she loved his van, too. They went everywhere together in it—Venice Beach, nice restaurants in Hollywood, and Las Vegas, where hotels like the Westward Ho, Stardust, and the MGM Grand put them up for free. The hotel managers loved having Dad's van covered in silver dollars parked outside their entrance. It was a great tourist attraction. Gretchen loved the attention almost as much as Dad.

On a hot autumn day without a cloud in the sky, I saw Dad watering the grass, wearing only his Speedos. I stood in the shadow of his van as I told him about my plan.

"The college is in Eureka, and I'll be going in the fall."

My plan was so out of the blue that it seemed to catch him by surprise.

"Okay."

"Do you like the idea?"

"You going to college is great."

"I have to do something after I graduate. It sounds like a lot of the expenses could be paid as long as I qualify for a government grant."

"How much will you need from me?"

"A little money here and there would be nice."

I didn't want to overshoot what I might need. Dad was generous, but we had never talked about funding college.

"I'll send you two bits a month."

Dad was cracking one of his standard jokes. Two bits was the equivalent of twenty-five cents. But it was his way of saying he could help. I took it as his blessing and that I wouldn't be on my own financially. At least I'd have him as a backup. I was so happy I skipped into the house.

That spring, I got an acceptance letter and learned I had qualified for a Pell grant. Since Dad wasn't always accurate with his income on his taxes, it was a hefty grant that would pay most of my expenses. It looked like I was really going to college!

When I went across the street to tell Mark about my plan, he was working under the hood of his truck. Since we were young kids, Mark and I had talked about moving away from the big city and making a life somewhere in the country where there weren't so many people and cars and smog everywhere. We hated that purple haze of pollution, which was normal in LA in the '80s. We often wondered if the air we breathed was killing us.

I was certain Mark would love my plan. He was always fishing and going on camping trips and spending time in the mountains. We went on day trips to Tujunga Canyon, Griffin Park, or fishing at Santa Monica Pier. Sometimes we bought a spot on a deep-sea fishing boat. Once we backpacked for three days in Kings Canyon and another time in Angeles Crest Forest. He would love Eureka.

"You'll never guess where I'm going in September. Northern California for college. I think I want to be a forest ranger."

"Forest ranger? Sure, I could see you as a forest ranger."

"What are you going to do after you graduate?"

"Maybe I'll start a landscape business."

"You should come to school with me. We could share a place and go to college together. We could be forest rangers together."

Mark scoffed.

"I don't know about a forest ranger, but it sounds like an interesting plan. Where is it?"

"Eureka. Near the redwoods and the ocean. It's beautiful."

"I know where you're talking about. It would be a great place to live."

Mark had been doing a lot of landscape work and had long considered starting his own business. I could tell he wasn't sold on the idea, but he seemed intrigued.

"Think about it. We could get out of Burbank. You've always wanted to, and I know your parents will help with money."

"Yeah, maybe."

"Staying here means living with our parents and finding a job or running a grueling business. You're too young for that."

"It does sound kinda grim."

"At least you know how to do something, Mark. Landscaping can make you pretty good money. But I don't know how to do anything. I need to go to college. I can't be a poor person."

Mark shut the hood of his truck and wiped his hands on his pants.

"Let's talk about it later this summer. It would be nice to live somewhere different."

I strolled back across the street, taking in the sight of Dad's van and the house. Maybe Mark would come with me after all. I couldn't wait to get to the redwood forest, and if Mark came along I wouldn't have to do it alone.

The last few months of high school were slow and hard. I got into a biology class and intermediate English, hoping they would prepare me for college. They were hard classes. I wasn't used to studying that much, but I was determined to graduate and be ready. I also made it to my seven o'clock first-period class every morning.

On graduation day, it was a sweltering one hundred degrees— perfect for a pool party. I had a whole clan of friends over to celebrate before the ceremony. Dad lounged around the pool and sunbathed like he always had. Most of my friends were used to seeing him with his bulging pectorals and bikini swimwear that left little to the imagination. But a couple kids had never seen him that way. They giggled when they looked at Dad in his Speedo. It embarrassed me, but there wasn't anything I could do about it. They could think whatever they wanted about Dad, who did whatever he felt like doing.

Tyler came over and gestured at Dad.

"Your dad is hot."

I could tell she was messing with me.

"Really. Your Dad is groovy, Steingold."

She laughed and took a swig of her beer. I looked at Dad getting out of the pool. With his perfect tan, he was like the male equivalent of having a hot mom, which was annoying.

"He's a little old for you, isn't he?"

Even though he was different from other dads, he had charisma, and everyone seemed to think well of him.

For graduation, I wore my bathing suit under my gown and didn't do a thing with my hair. I had crazy hair, ropey and wild, and it smelled of chlorine. I hadn't changed much since grade school. I didn't care what I looked like that day. I was moving away and going to college. That's all that mattered. I was a happy, content, soul.

One day in the middle of July, I saw Mark sitting on our porch. When he heard me, he sat up and smiled. He seemed animated about something. I wondered if he had been smoking pot. Mark loved pot. His clear, big blue eyes said he hadn't. Mark was on a natural high.

"Guess what? I'm going to Eureka with you."

I could hardly believe my ears. Flabbergasted, I gave Mark the biggest hug ever. I skipped around the porch, cheering and pumping my fist into the air. My best friend in the world was moving away to college with me.

Mark knew that if he didn't get out of town now, he might not be able to later. Burbank had been a great city for us to grow up in, but it was time to go. Mark said he still wanted to do some kind of landscaping business, but he wanted to keep his options open.

"Who knows? I might like college and get a degree."

36

Into the Woods

Mark and I left home in early September 1981. Dad had given me his Buick Riviera, but I left it home because it was terrible on gas, and Mark and I wanted to make the six-hundred-mile drive together in his Chevy truck.

As Dad saw us off, he handed me two one-hundred-dollar bills.

"Don't spend it all in one place."

I thanked him profusely, stuffed the money in my pocket, and gave him a big hug. Money was going to be tight, even with my grant and the Lilliputian savings I had stored in my dresser. I couldn't access the dog-bite money until I was eighteen, which was months away, so the money from Dad really helped. I didn't want to work, so I could concentrate on my classes.

"I'm pretty sure you've cost me the most out of you three kids."

Dad never stopped ribbing me.

"Probably."

I smiled meekly at his joke. It was probably true.

"So, you don't know where you are going to live yet?"

"We're going to find a place once we're there."

"How long of a drive is it?"

"Maybe twelve hours or so."

"That's a pretty good long drive."

Dad scratched his unshaven chin, looking somewhat worried. I hadn't told him about the details of my plan. He was taking this last opportunity to find out what I was doing, and he seemed uneasy. His youngest was moving away to college and it showed on his face. Knowing that gave me a good feeling, affirmation of his love.

"I'll be fine, Dad."

He rubbed me on the back.

"I know you will."

Mark made a point to shake Dad's hand.

"See you, Ernie."

"You take care of my girl, Mark."

Then Dad looked at me again.

"I love you."

He kissed me on the cheek.

"And keep your nose clean. You hear?"

"I love you, too, and I'll do my best."

Dad closed the door for me and made sure it was shut good and tight. From the sidewalk, he waved, and as Mark hit the gas, I got one last glimpse of Dad and the van. It was time for a new adventure!

The drive was smooth and uneventful. A couple days later, we found a ranch house to rent in King Salmon, two miles from campus. It had three bedrooms, a big kitchen, living room, and the front yard was a huge gravel parking lot. The house sat on the main road, across the street from a power plant. The huge nuclear stacks were visible through the window. I didn't like the sight of them, but I was glad to hear that the nuclear part of the plant had been inactive since 1976.

Our house was nifty. From the front porch you could hear ocean waves hitting the shore. But it was foggy by the bay and often felt dark, dismal, and isolated. It usually took all morning for the sun to break through. But King Salmon turned out to be a beautiful place. We had the beach and open fields with cows.

We didn't have much furniture, so we went to the local thrift store and bought mattresses, a table and chairs for the kitchen, and a couch for the living room.

Our landlord, Captain Ole, lived next door. He was a deep-sea fishing captain and had a dog he always carried around. He parked his big old fishing boat next to his house on a canal that led to the bay.

King Salmon beach was only a half-mile around the bend, but we mostly drove there. All the streets were named for a fish—cod, herring, sole, and crab. Each was lined by a canal full of boats. It felt a little shabby but decent, with quaint cottages and trailer parks. The boat ramp and minimart were active with men in fishing gear, smoking cigarettes, and cajoling one another. I smelled barbecue, and a couple riding bikes smiled at me. A few people on the beach played soccer, and the sun felt nice and warm. I wondered if life could get any better. If it wasn't for the fog and rain that was so legendary, it would have been a great place to live permanently.

Mark's dog, Bo, jumped out of the truck and ran up to a guy who lived right near us on Herring Street.

"I'm Mark, and this is Tracy. No relations."

Sometimes, Mark and I were mistaken as a couple, and he must have wanted to make it clear with our new neighbor that we were not together like that. He usually only did that with pretty girls, telling them I was his sister.

Paul had a lumpy nose and black flowing hair that looked freshly brushed. I thought he was in his mid-twenties. He went to College of the Redwoods part-time and worked at the local hospital as a nursing assistant. He had a calm, friendly vibe, and I liked him right away, especially after he pulled out a joint and asked if we wanted to smoke with him.

We smoked the entire thing. The pot was strong, and I felt the effects quickly. The buzz was pleasant, and the beach was calming and beautiful as the three of us talked and threw a piece of driftwood for Bo.

Paul told us about the marijuana growing in Humboldt County, which was the heartland for high-quality pot farming in California. Apparently, there was a strong counterculture that Mark and I had yet to experience. We had seen plenty of hippie types and Harleys around town, but Paul seemed enthusiastic about the unique nature of where we now lived.

"Go up to Arcata. You'd think you were back in the sixties."

He told us about the magic mushrooms growing in the fields around the power plant. They grew naturally around cow pies and Humboldt County had a perfect climate for them.

"I'll take you out some time. The psilocybin in the shrooms are amazing and free."

A week later, just before our first week of college, Mark put a pot roast in the oven and the house smelled amazing. We cooked everything from scratch; I never knew Mark could cook so well. I didn't do much outside of the basics, like Hamburger Helper, scrambled eggs, fried pork chop, or a steak. Nothing fancy like Mark. He baked a snapper he caught in a river, fried a battered chicken on the stove, and made our famous cowboy sandwiches for breakfast, just as he did when we were little. All you had to do was cut a cup-sized hole out of a buttered piece of bread, throw it on a skillet and drop an egg in the middle. It was easy and fast and light on our budget.

"Let's go to the beach and watch the sunset until the roast is done."

Like Bo, I was onboard. Nothing was better than a walk on the beach. That day, we practically had it to ourselves. The evening air was warm, and a light breeze wafted off the soft churning surf. It felt like our very own piece of paradise.

As we watched the sun set in streams of brilliant reds and oranges, I thought about my new freedom. All the friends I left behind, and everything else so familiar. It was up to me now to make choices in my life. Dad would be there to fall back on if something went wrong, and I knew he wouldn't let me starve to death. Ultimately, though, I knew it was up to me. I had the whole world in my hands and felt like I could be anything I wanted.

When we got back to the truck, we saw a couple bearded men smoking a joint. These guys wore scraggly flannel shirts, worn leather boots, and their hair looked like it hadn't been brushed in a week. The skinny dark-haired one with high, sharp cheekbones and wide slitty eyes greeted us and he smiled at me. I smiled back, even though he seemed kind of sinister as he looked me over like I was at a cattle auction.

The blond guy offered us his joint, which I declined because I didn't want to put my mouth on anything these guys had touched, and I didn't want to start feeling paranoid. Those two guys were already giving me the creeps. Mark took a small hit and quickly passed it back. I could tell he was just being cordial, and he asked them if they lived in the neighborhood.

"We're living in my truck right now, looking for work, saving our money."

Cheekbones took another hit as the blond guy asked where we lived. I turned to Mark, trying to let him know *not* to tell them where we live. Thank God he wasn't stupid. I certainly didn't want these guys knowing where they could find us.

I'd never met a homeless person, but my instinct was to be brief and not too friendly. I didn't want them ending up on our doorstep or asking to sleep in our front room and having to tell them no. I threw a stick for Bo and headed to the passenger side of Mark's truck, hoping he would take the hint. Within five minutes we were home and eating pot roast. Life was good and our first day of college was in the morning.

School was just an exit south down Highway 101. Eureka was two exits in the other direction. When I didn't ride with Mark to campus I took the bus, just a short walk from our house.

The Avenue of the Giants, home of the biggest redwood trees in the world, was just a hop skip and a jump away. The forest had endless places to hike and rivers to explore. I often trekked the trails, picking mushrooms like chanterelles and the magic ones, too.

I told Dad how beautiful the area was and how he should visit, but he never seemed to consider making the trip.

37

Party House

I met people from New York, Oregon, Southern California, even a guy from Kenya whose name was Osu, a slender, dark fellow who spoke English with a strong accent. He was in my American history class, and we talked a few times about the Puritans and the similarities they had to the founders of his country.

When Osu learned of my last name, he asked if I was Jewish, and when I told him I was, his eyes opened wide with alarm. He huddled up close and pointed with his long bony finger.

"The Palestinian students here . . . if they see you, they kill you."

I studied Osu's face, not knowing what to make of him. He was dead serious. At the time, Palestinian terrorists were killing Israelis. Not a month went by without a bomb being detonated in a cafe in Jerusalem, but there was no threat of that in Northern California.

Osu warned me again.

"They will shoot you and kill you. Be very careful."

A guy sitting next to us, who seemed to know Osu, started laughing.

"Those kids aren't going to kill anyone."

I was blown away by Osu's concern. In Burbank, kids never gave me a hard time for being Jewish. I'm not sure they even knew; it never came up. I was pretty naive to the prejudices against Jews that lingered around the world. I felt fortunate to never experience the hate Osu was talking about.

It was easy to make friends at college. But following Dad's advice and "keeping my nose clean" wasn't in the cards. The people I seemed to be drawn to were partiers and pot smokers who played hackie sac and didn't do their homework. As for classes, I learned quickly that I had to work a little harder to get by. College wasn't like public school, where C's and D's sufficed. I did pretty well for the most part, but I wasn't bound for academic greatness where scholarships would abound. I wasn't driven to worm through books and spend all my time studying to get excellent grades. That time would come, but for now I was preoccupied with meeting new people and having adventures.

Mark and I met a guy a little older than us named Chris Payne. He was a beachcomber, surfer type from Southern California who lived in a motorhome and had long luscious blond hair. Chris trekked around barefoot and seemed to be friends with everyone. He played drums in a local band that sounded pretty good.

A month later, Chris appeared on our front steps, and I invited him in.

"I thought I'd stop by and see what's going on. Nice pad you got here."

Chris helped himself to a quick tour of the place and sat between us on the couch.

"This would be a great place for a party. It's like a cathedral in here."

Chris was right. The living room was huge. The floors were hardwood, so if we had a party, we wouldn't have to worry about people spoiling the carpet. We could fit fifty people if they were standing, plus there was plenty of room outside to park.

"I could have my band here by the weekend."

Mark seemed distracted by his textbook, and he loved his classes. I, on the other hand, loved the idea of a party with a live band, especially if they were half decent.

"That would be fun."

"My girlfriend sings vocals and has some hot friends who will show up."

Mark didn't need much encouragement. If there was a party, he was onboard. He still had his girlfriend back home, but they had partly broken up. For Mark, the hot girl angle was an added bonus.

"Sure, we can all pitch in for a keg. As long as Tracy's in, I'm in."

I was definitely in. All I hoped for were lots of good-looking boys.

On Saturday night, it seemed like people showed up from everywhere. Besides fellow students and Chris's friends, they were mostly Humboldt County folk who wore Birkenstocks and corduroy jeans and loved smoking pot and talking about greenhouses and organics.

Chris introduced Mark and I to Charlie Wood, who showed up with a few of his huge biker friends. Charlie was a cross between a biker and a hippy, with long, fluffy black hair, a gray beard, round puppy eyes, and a silver-studded earring in his right ear. He was much older than everyone else and walked with a slight limp from crashing his Harley on Highway 101.

The day before, Chris came over to set up his drums and we talked about all kinds of things. He told me about his recently divorced parents in Newport Beach. He loved to brag about his dad who was a rocket scientist and worked for McDonald Douglas. According to Chris, his dad was the smartest man at the company, maybe the entire world. He was paying his son's way through college and had provided the Winnebago Chris was living in.

I decided to brag about my dad, too. I showed Chris two pictures of Dad with his van.

"This is your dad's van? I've seen this in Venice. God I love this. Your dad is famous."

Once I got away from home and had distanced myself from the van, I discovered I liked telling people about Dad and his crazy creation.

I found a new sense of pride in it. Who else had a van like that? It was a great conversation piece and seemed to bring joy to people.

Charlie and I listened to the band play another Fleetwood Mac song, which they played almost exclusively along with a few Neil Young songs. The two women had pleasant voices and sang mostly in key. They reminded me of Stevie Nicks and Christine McVie. I think they were trying to be like them. Once *Dreams* was over, the bikers followed me and Charlie into the kitchen to get some beer.

Charlie wanted to hear more about Dad's van.

"I'll be right back."

"Is it okay if I use your phone to call my wife?"

"As long as she doesn't live in Cucamonga."

That was a saying Dad sometimes used for any place far away.

"She's right down the street, but she may be on her way over here."

Next thing I knew, Charlie introduced me to his wife, Beatrice. She had long silver hair and wore a knee-length crocheted poncho that swayed when she moved. She and Charlie lived on the other side of the canal and had two grown children. They made jewelry and sold it to retail stores around Eureka. The three of us sat at the kitchen table, looking at pictures of Dad.

"So, this is what your dad drove while you were growing up?"

Charlie seemed fascinated.

"I'm afraid so."

I felt myself cringe at the thought of everyone staring at me.

Charlie giggled and shook his head. "Musta been rough."

Charlie said metals were a passion for him. He worked with silver and pewter, but he loved the look of the brass on Dad's van.

"My station wagon could use a hood ornament. What a great idea."

I liked people who liked Dad's van; some hated it. They thought it was ugly or vulgar. When Dad was interviewed, he shared how it antagonized some people and how it brought out a mean streak in them. Sometimes, people flipped him the bird or screamed at him, calling the van "an ugly piece of shit." Dad always smiled and waved and never seemed rattled in his cool response.

"Hang loose, brother. Have a good day."

Charlie was about Dad's age, but he talked to me like an adult. I could say just about anything without worrying about offending him or shocking him. Charlie became like a favorite uncle to Mark and me. He stopped by the house now and then and sometimes gave me a ride to school in his Ford Falcon station wagon. He was always kind and thoughtful, and it didn't seem to faze him that we were teenagers fresh out of high school.

The bikers with Charlie stayed in the kitchen with the keg. They wore leather pants and had their hair pulled back in ponytails. Each of them had a black leather jacket with an insignia on the back I didn't recognize. Did they belong to a conventional biker club or were they members of a Hells Angels type gang? They were certainly a different breed of biker than my dad ever was, but they didn't make me feel uncomfortable. They were polite, probably the best mannered people at the whole party.

Cheekbones was not as well mannered. He lumbered into the kitchen. His clothes were smudged badly with dirt and his pants dragged on the floor. He ignored the bikers and went straight for the beer. I watched him fill a cup from the keg and lick the foam from the bottom of his mustache. He turned and caught my eye with that sneering smile of his. Before he walked away, I could have sworn his eyes deliberately gazed at my crotch. The guy was a creep.

For a couple months, we had a party at our house almost every weekend. At first, Mark and I loved it. We had Chris's band a few times and lots of fun people. But after a while, the fun wore off because we grew tired of cleaning up after them. Plus, it wasn't the smartest idea to make our place a college party house. All sorts of people trampled through, and for some reason, Mark kept inviting Cheekbones. We never had problems with people or the police like I had experienced in Burbank. People went home when the party was over. For me, the only trouble came toward the end of the semester.

38
Cheekbones

It was a thick cloudy day and the rain had just slowed to a sprinkle when I got off the bus after school. I walked home as I usually did. Mark's truck was parked in a massive pothole filled with rainwater. It had broken down and he couldn't afford to get it fixed, so both of us were taking the bus.

When I reached the front steps, Cheekbones was standing at the bottom.

"Well, hello there."

His voice startled me. He seemed to come out of nowhere.

"Mark's still at school."

I dug in my backpack for my key.

"I wasn't looking for Mark."

By the time I glanced back, Cheekbones grabbed my arm and twisted it back. My backpack fell and thudded on the landing. I was stunned. I turned as hard as I could and broke loose from his grasp. I got a couple steps away, but Cheekbones was quick and forced me down on the steps. I could smell his bad breath.

"Get the fuck off of me you creep!"

He pressed his body on me and groped my crotch with such force that it hurt. He didn't let up. I heard a car drive by, but it kept going.

A ferocious anger grew inside me. I was being sexually assaulted. I knew this was something most women in the world went through at least once in their lifetime, and my turn was now, in broad daylight.

I couldn't knee him in the groin like Dad had counseled me to do if I got into a situation like this. But I was able to bend one knee and wedge my thigh between us. I got one arm mostly free, too. My days of throwing the shot put and lifting weights weren't that far behind me; I was still strong as ever. With one swift jerk, I extended my arms and pushed my legs with all my might. Cheekbones practically flew through the air as I launched him off me. He landed snap-dab in the middle of a huge puddle at the bottom of the steps. It was an image I would never forget. He stood and swiped at his wet pants, shaking his head from the humiliation. He was soaked.

"You're not worth it."

He waved his hand at me in disgust.

A week later, I came home and found Cheekbones and Mark drinking coffee in our kitchen. I had told Mark what Cheekbones had done. Did he not understand the gravity of the attack? Why else would he let him into our house? Mark was clueless.

"He can't be in here, Mark."

Cheekbones looked at him.

"He's got to get out of the house. Now!"

Mark looked at Cheekbones. "You better go."

Not long after that, Charlie invited Mark and me to a biker bar where he was celebrating Beatrice's birthday. I thought it was a strange invitation, considering we were both underage, but I was happy to go.

The place was hopping with bikers and their tattooed girlfriends, wives, or what have you. Charlie, Beatrice, and I got a table across from the bar, and he poured beer from a pitcher. Charlie and Beatrice's friends came over to wish her a happy birthday. I was clearly the odd girl out. I didn't wear leather, tight jeans, or pink lipstick like the other women, and I must have been the youngest person in the tavern. If it wasn't for Charlie and his wife, I would have felt entirely out of place.

When I went to the bar to refill our bowl of pretzels, I saw good-for-nothing Cheekbones glaring at me with his ugly grin. I looked away hoping he'd leave me alone, but he came right up close and leaned in when he spoke.

"Well look who's here."

"Get away from me."

"What are you doing in this bar anyway? Aren't you a bit young?"

I raised the bowl to the woman bartender.

"Could I get some pretzels please?"

I felt reassured that Charlie and Beatrice were not far away, but when I turned to go back to the table, Cheekbones grabbed my arm. Before I knew what happened, three guys came out of nowhere, grabbed Cheekbones, and ran out with him to the parking lot. It was like something you'd see in a movie. I was stunned. The bikers must have watched Cheekbones badgering women the whole time he was at there. I had heard about bikers being protective of women, that if someone disrespected their wife or girlfriend, they were likely to beat the shit out of them. Boy, did I love bikers!

I didn't see Cheekbones again that night, but that wasn't the end of him. His sorry ass came around the house a couple days later. He had a black eye, and his socket was red with broken blood vessels. His lip was split, too. I tried not to smile at the sight of him. I loved that he got the shit knocked out of him by a bunch of bikers. He deserved it. I would have slammed the door in his face if Mark hadn't been home.

"What do you want?"

"I'm looking for Mark."

"Mark! Someone's at the door for you."

I didn't take my eyes off Cheekbones as I spoke to Mark.

"He can't come into our house."

I don't know what Cheekbones wanted that day, but I never saw him again.

39
Homesick

Mark and I decided to move out of King Salmon. After the Cheekbones incident, I felt unsafe there. Even with bikers watching my back, I didn't know what kind of psychopath he might be, and I didn't want him to know where I lived.

Mark wasn't as concerned, which I never understood. He seemed unable to relate to my fear of being assaulted again. He brushed the attack off as a one-time thing, which was very aggravating. Were men naturally so complacent about sexual assault?

Luckily, Mark was tired of living in a college party house, too, so we rented a two-bedroom cottage down the highway in Fortuna. The place was smaller and a hundred dollars cheaper, situated in a group of other cottages in a quaint rural neighborhood just a quarter mile from the highway. I could catch the bus to school easily. It was perfect. We had neighbors close by, but not too close, and we could see green pastures and sheep outside the kitchen window.

On our first day there, a guy named Robert knocked on our front door to ask if we wanted to come over for a welcome barbecue. He was a young man who lived across the driveway with his twin brother, Richard.

That evening, we sat on their patio next to a beautiful vegetable garden. I thought Robert was cute and felt attracted to him, but it never went further than that. They were twenty-two and studying engineering with plans to transfer to Humboldt State to finish their degrees. They had grown up in Nigeria and their parents were rich oil executives who still lived there. They supported their sons with a generous monthly stipend that allowed them an extravagant lifestyle. They had nice trucks, all sorts of guns and electronics, and the food was endless.

After we smoked some weed and had a few beers, Robert told me about the pot he and his brother grew on unclaimed land in the woods near Dinsmore. When they cultivated their crop, they took shotguns, just in case they ran into any poachers or police. I gave him a sideways glance when I heard that. Were they going to shoot a cop or someone else over a cash crop?

By the time we got shish kabobs on the grill, a gal who looked like a '60s flower child emerged from a nearby house wearing a long flowing dress, hooped earrings, and silver jewelry with gems around her wrists. She had red hair, a freckled complexion, and glassy blue eyes. Beth had a Coors in one hand and a large bowl of green salad in the other. I noticed a reefer nestled against her right ear.

"Fresh out of the garden."

I guessed she was talking about the salad, not the joint. But Beth wasn't all Humboldt hippy. She was a forest ranger who had gotten her forestry degree like I wanted to.

"How do you like working in forestry?"

"The money is shit." She pulled the joint from her ear and lit it up.

"It's a great job, don't get me wrong, but it can be tough paying my bills."

She specialized in managing coastal redwood trees, so she didn't work for the state park or wear a gun like some rangers. I thought carrying a gun would be a cool part of the job. I liked the idea of protecting the forest and the people in it. Beth wore a uniform and a cool looking hat, and she sometimes drove an official green truck home from work.

Beth was a great neighbor. Sometimes we drove into town to get groceries, and I went to her house to study while she did her chores. Whenever she talked about her forestry gig, though, I wasn't impressed. Her job entailed a lot of paperwork and gathering data for the National Forest Service. The areas she worked in were stunning, but she spent most of her time at a desk, and most of it was solitary. I wasn't so sure I would like that, not to mention the low wages. A comfortable salary was important to me.

Mark and the twins hit it off because they loved fishing and four-wheeling their trucks in the mountains, shooting clay pigeons at Swimmers Delight up Highway 36. They showed Mark their marijuana plot, and he became fascinated by the idea of cultivating his own.

I didn't appreciate the brothers as much as Mark. One day, they pulled up in their truck and Richard was obviously drunk. I was glad Mark wasn't with them. We never drove drunk, and Mark knew better.

"Get the guns, Robert."

Richard stumbled up the steps to their cottage.

"I got to take a piss." Robert was laughing.

"We sure got those fuckers running,"

"They must have felt the wind of the buckshot flying past their heads."

I asked Robert who was running.

"Some fucking kids that were two clicks from our farm."

The brothers called their weed spot in the woods "the farm," as if they owned the land.

"You shot at kids?"

"We didn't hit them."

"You better not have."

Good Lord! Who are these guys?

When I got back inside, I thought longingly of being home in Burbank. It was the first time I felt homesick. Dad and I talked on the phone every couple of weeks. I especially liked it when he rang me up. It felt good to know he was thinking about me, and hearing his voice eased my worries. I enjoyed hearing about his van adventures, how he had been on *Real People* and met Sara Purcell when she came to the house. I told him what I'd been up to, like visiting Avenue of the Giants, and that Mark and I drove his truck through a live redwood tree. Dad seemed genuinely interested in my stories, and I thought we had better conversations on the phone than we ever had at home, face-to-face. I asked him to visit, but he didn't really respond.

He called one day with big news.

"I'm getting married to Gretchen."

The wedding was planned for May, and he wanted me to come. He promised me that this marriage was the real deal.

"I'd shoot myself in the foot before I get another annulment."

Ten years had passed since Mom died. I thought Dad was long overdue to have a new wife. He told me Gretchen was finally the perfect woman. I was glad for him and told him I wouldn't miss it.

Two months later, when I sat in Dad's living room before the ceremony, I couldn't get his last wedding out of my head. Ginger and her guests were different, of course, but it still felt like *deja vu.*

Practically our entire family was there. Steve and Allison, most of my aunts and uncles, two of my cousins, and some of Dad's Bahai friends. Gretchen had her two kids and her brother, Virgil, as well as a few others. The man conducting the ceremony was the same Bahai minister that married Dad three years earlier.

Dad wore the same black-and-white speckled tweed jacket and his silver dollar belt buckle. His new bride was a breed of her own. She shared no resemblance to Ginger, at least as far as I could tell. Gretchen wore a figure fitting, off-white lace dress that stopped short of the knee. She was pale white compared to Dad's bronzed skin, and she was practically as big of a ham as Dad. She fawned and cooed at him throughout the short ceremony. I saw her wink at her daughter after she and Dad kissed.

Dad was incredibly happy, and it showed. He shook everyone's hand and kept smooching his new wife whenever he could. He was head over heels for Gretchen, and it was nice to see him so happy, but I couldn't help feeling a bit of anxiety about the whole thing.

I didn't know Gretchen very well. When I lived at home while Dad dated her, I hardly came in contact with her. I went out with them for a meal or two, but most of our contact was in passing. At the reception, she seemed thoughtful and polite, serving people drinks and putting out a lovely spread of food. But that day I discovered that Gretchen wasn't always the easiest person to get along with; lots of things were about to change.

We were in the dining room, sipping cocktails, and socializing. The dining room had the same stereo system Dad had wired to two huge speakers that hung on the living room wall. It was a great sound, and you could crank it up loud. Dad never minded loud music if he wasn't watching television. He sometimes played music of his own, too.

Steve put on a Boston album and turned it up enough to hear without being too loud to have a comfortable conversation. But Gretchen hurried into the dining room and turned the volume so low it was inaudible. I thought she was going to make a sentimental toast, but that wasn't the case. She was irritated.

"Now that's another thing that stops today."

I caught a tone of annoyance in her voice. I looked at Allison and we both thought the same thing. *Holy crap! Do we now have an evil stepmother?*

Later that evening, the three of us talked outside before going our separate ways. Steve was living at Dad's again, but things weren't too smooth since Gretchen had moved in. Last week, he walked into his bedroom and found a pile of dirty dishes on his bed.

"I mean, how odd is that? Dirty dishes on my bed? I asked Dad and Gretchen about it."

Apparently, Gretchen was teaching Steve a lesson. She hated dirty dishes left for her to clean, so that's how she complained.

"If you leave dirty dishes, that's what you're going to get."

My sister Allison was baffled. "Who does that?"

I had an answer. "A mean person."

I didn't plan to be around much, but it was scary to think I would have to answer to Gretchen and walk a fine line when I was home. She was right. A lot of things were changing. Thankfully, I was going back to school.

40
Out of the Woods

I wasn't thrilled being a forestry major. I was enrolled in a land management course, timber harvesting, and wild land fire control. I didn't like any of those classes and the last thing I wanted to do was fight wildfires. My reaction surprised me. I discovered that I didn't care that much about land rights and the logistics of clear-cutting private lands. I loved the forest, but I didn't want to spend all my time thinking about it.

On top of these academic woes, the boys in those classes were a turn off. They wore ugly flannel shirts, scruffy uneven beards, and it felt like a boys' club. I was one of three girls. I tried to talk with one guy who I thought was cute, but he wouldn't give me the time of day. I'd never seen boys so awkward around girls. I didn't make one friend in those classes. Plus, the forest rangers' low salary weighed heavy on my mind. I started to think I wasn't going to get anything I wanted in that field.

If anything saved my spring quarter, it was joining the track-and-field team. I did pretty well in high school, and I was even better in college. My meets took place all over Northern California. It was nice to be part of a team sport again, and we had a blast going to meets on the weekends. I threw the shot and the javelin and broke the College of the Redwoods women's shotput record, with a throw of thirty-six feet, eight inches. During meets, I often thought of Dad pulling up in his van to see me throw. I didn't miss the van, but I sure missed him watching me.

By the time school ended, I decided forestry was not for me. I considered joining a police academy or majoring in physical education, but I couldn't see myself working in those capacities, especially becoming a cop. I dreamed of being a detective and thought I would make a good one, but being a cop meant following lots of rules, but I wasn't the greatest rule follower, especially if I thought the rules were stupid. I didn't trust cops for the most part, either. The ones I'd come in contact with never seemed to be entirely truthful, and that always rubbed me the wrong way.

Being a full-time student, I still didn't have a job. The government paid my tuition, and I was getting a small Social Security survivor benefit from losing my mom, but I had no other income. Dad had been sending me fifty dollars every month, but since he married Gretchen, those checks had stopped. I worried that the cost of living would tap out my dog-bite savings account. I didn't want to waste my money on classes that wouldn't lead to a viable degree. I needed to decide what to do with my life—and fast.

During finals week, I spoke to a recruiter who made the Air Force sound ten times better than the Navy. I wouldn't have to stay on ships for days or even weeks at a time, like in the Navy. In the Air Force, I could learn about computers and acquire skills I couldn't find at a community college; I would even get paid while doing it. I also didn't have to worry about a ridiculous weight limit. Plus, because of track and field, I was in the best shape of my life, lifting weights and running religiously. I was thinner than before and could probably get in easily.

I had many sleepless nights thinking about everything. Summer was approaching and I was already planning on returning to Burbank. Did I want to come back to Eureka after that? I was spinning my wheels and had no clear direction. Things that had happened there bothered me as well, like Cheekbones attacking me, and the twin brothers brandishing their guns. The constant gloomy weather was enough to drive anyone away.

The rest of my dog-bite money was in the First National Bank in downtown Burbank. When I turned eighteen, I had a total of seventy-eight hundred dollars in the account. Dad had talked me into leaving most of it there so it could collect interest. I had already used some to buy a Chevy truck and a Yamaha 250 dirt bike. The Buick Riviera Dad had given me was in Burbank, but I didn't want to drive that old gas hog. All the same, I didn't see the sense in taking the bus or bumming rides. The motorcycle fit perfectly in the back of the truck, and riding on the beach dunes was a blast, but it wasn't the best use of my money.

When Dad stopped sending me money each month, it boggled my mind. Apparently, Gretchen forbid it.

"I don't give my kids money." That's what she told Dad.

Hearing him tell me this didn't sit well. I was in college. Her kids weren't. What was the logic? Was it just greed? I was beginning to feel negative toward Gretchen, and I would be living with her in Dad's house, at least through the summer—a daunting thought. That's partly why the Air Force appealed to me. I had no idea what turning my life over to the armed forces would mean, but it seemed like a viable solution. I could get away from home and learn a marketable skill. I didn't know what, but it would be something.

I decided to go back home for the summer, take it easy for a while, and pursue enlisting. I told Mark I was moving out in June and not coming back.

41

Locked Out

Summer was my favorite time of year. With school out and the sun blazing down, I planned to spend my time lazing by Dad's pool. I left Eureka in the middle of the night and drove my truck twelve hours straight to Burbank, carrying everything I owned. When I arrived around three in the afternoon, I was hoping to unload my things and swim. At that time, still a lazy, unmotivated eighteen-year-old, I just wanted to goof around and enjoy myself. I even considered calling a friend to see if she could come over and drink some beers with me by the pool. It was summer break. But as soon as I got back to Burbank, I realized nothing was quite right.

The van was gone. Gretchen's VW Rabbit was parked against the gate to the pool. There was no way to access it except by climbing over her car. The front door was locked, and my key didn't work. *Why is that brown Rabbit piece of shit parked like that?* It seemed like I was being purposely locked out of the house and the yard. I had told Dad I was coming home. He said he and Gretchen were going to Las Vegas, but that they were supposed to be back. If I couldn't get into the house, at least I could sit by the pool and wait for them.

That's when Grace, who lived next to Mark, walked up. Whenever I saw her, I thought of strawberries. Mark and I ate lots of strawberries from her garden. She never minded. Grace was a nice lady. She was also the tallest woman I'd ever known, over six feet, with thick glasses and a high-pitched voice I'd always known as kind. She spoke with a slight Texas drawl.

"Hello Tracy. Whatcha up to?"

"You wouldn't happen to have a key to my dad's house, would you?"

I knew Grace kept a house key for Dad in case of emergency. She also fed the cat when he was away.

"I'm not supposed to let anyone in. I just came to feed the cat."

"Not even me? I'm staying here over the summer."

"I don't think they want anyone in the house while they're gone. That's what they said. I'm not supposed to let anyone in."

I could see she felt bad telling me that. Grace had watched me grow up. I thought about asking her to make an exception, but I didn't want to make her repeat saying no to me. It was odd waiting outside while Grace fed the cat. A couple minutes later, Hoover rubbed up against me and I stroked his back while I watched Grace cross the street.

"They should be back soon."

I could tell she felt sorry for me and probably a little guilty. I wasn't mad at Grace; she was just following directions. For all I knew, Gretchen had told her not to let me into the house. *Why did they lock me out of the yard? Can't they have at least let me use the pool?*

Steve and Allison lived nearby in Burbank, and Allison said I could stay with them if I wanted, and that the couch was quite comfortable. Thanks to them, I had somewhere to fall back on. But I was looking forward to staying at Dad's through the summer and sleeping in my old room. This wasn't the welcome I expected.

I watched Grace go back into her house. Mark was still in Eureka and wasn't due back in Burbank for another month. But his parents were home, so I figured I could probably spend the rest of the day with them and wait for Dad.

Mark's mom was happy to see me. She licked her fingers and waved me in. The house smelled of fried chicken, and I had dinner with them and hung out into the evening. It was comfortable over there, but I wanted to go home. Every few minutes I checked to see if

Dad had pulled in; it was eight o'clock when I heard the faint ringing chimes of the van. I jumped up off the couch and saw Dad pulling his van into the driveway.

Dad was happy to see me. He put down what he was carrying and gave me a big hug and kissed me on the lips like he always did when we'd been apart for an extended time. He started going on about what a great time he and Gretchen had in Las Vegas. The Westward Ho Hotel had put them up for five days, food and lodging included. Dad parked his van in front of the hotel because management must have figured if a guy could waste thousands of silver dollars riveting them onto his van, it had to inspire others to slip their coins into the slot machines. Dad said the van looked jazzy out there on the strip and that loads of people flocked to it. Even after the long drive back, Dad was still giddy with excitement.

Gretchen seemed to be in a good mood, too. She gave me a soft peck on my cheek. She'd never done that before, but I liked the friendly gesture and it erased some of the bad feelings I had toward her.

"You want something to eat Tracy?"

"I ate at Mark's house."

"Well, that was nice of them."

"I've been over there the past three hours. My key didn't work, and I wanted to use the pool, but the car was in the way."

"We didn't want anyone using the pool."

Clearly that *anyone* included me. I didn't feel like I should make it a big deal. Maybe Dad forgot what day I was arriving.

"I was surprised is all. Are there pool hoppers around the neighborhood now?"

My attempt at making a joke fell flat. No one laughed.

I had the house to myself that first full day. Gretchen worked full time as a bookkeeper while Dad was at his vacuum store. By the time they got home, I was still out by the pool, reading a magazine and listening to the radio. It had been a perfect summer day in Southern California.

Gretchen put on her swimsuit and brought out a tall pitcher of iced tea. She casually turned the volume down on the radio and handed me a cup.

"What a beautiful day."

She seemed polite and cheerful. I was curious about Gretchen and happy to have her at the pool with me, hoping she and I could be friends. I was giving her the benefit of the doubt, which we both deserved. For the most part, it went splendidly.

Gretchen was quite a character—funny, kindhearted, and seemingly decent. As we waded in the pool together, she told me stories about her adventures with Dad, like when they parked the van in front of Mann's Chinese Theater and droves of people came up to talk to them. The crowd got so big that a cop told them to move along, that they were causing a traffic jam. Then she told me about helping Dad dye his hair with black spray paint. That sounded exactly like something Dad would do. Apparently, he thought his newest hair piece had too much gray, so he thought he would spray a little black on it. Big mistake. It made his toupee rock hard and stiff. Gretchen said the only thing that removed it was kerosene. Since his hair piece was sutured to his head, she had to pour it on his head, which sounded horrifying and dangerous, but everything had worked out.

From there, the conversation went downhill. I don't know what caused the change. Maybe it was a song on the radio. That's how strange it was. Gretchen wouldn't stop asking me about my plans. Dad must have told her I was leaving college to join the Air Force. For some reason, she thought that was a longshot.

"The Navy didn't let you in because you were overweight, right? What if you don't get into the Air Force?"

My heart pounded when she said that. I didn't like her reference to my weight. But I had to agree with her about the enlistment. I hadn't heard from my recruiter in a couple weeks, and I had doubts about ever joining the military. To deflect from talking about it, I told Gretchen I wasn't staying long and that she didn't need to worry about it.

"I'll be gone by the end of summer."

By her expression, she didn't like my timeline. She went on about the Hawaii trip she and Dad were planning, and how she didn't like the idea of me being in the house alone. I didn't understand her concern. *What's the big deal about me being here when they're not around? What does she think I was going to do, go through her underwear drawer?* She was annoying me, and I would have loved to say that, but I didn't dare. The last thing I needed was to get Gretchen's panties in a bunch. I had no idea what Dad would do if I got her mad.

42

Me? A Nurse?

I got bored hanging around Dad's house. Most of my friends worked, or I had lost touch with them. But I did meet up with my old friend Betty May who was now married to her high school sweetheart, Dan, the hoodlum who was at Pam's house when her dad pulled a gun on us.

Betty's Uncle Reiny joined us at a barbecue. He liked talking on CB channels, using the handle Monkey Wrench because he worked on planes at the Lockheed airfield. He invited Betty, Dan, and me to join him and his fiancé on a trip to Owens River for the Fourth of July weekend.

"If I remember right, Tracy, you're a motorcycle rider?

"I sure am. I have my own 250 Yamaha dirt bike, too."

"Well, I'm bringing two little dirt bikes and you're welcome to bring yours, too."

He was meeting up with a couple of his buddies and their families. There would be motorcycles, inner tubes, and plenty of beer. I was ecstatic. The trip would be a perfect way to spend my time away from Dad's.

When I met Reiny's fiancé, Leora, she told me he had told her all kinds of nice things about me. I blushed. As always, I felt embarrassed by compliments, and undeserving. But I thanked her. I had learned from a camp counselor to thank people for compliments.

"It's rude not to acknowledge kindness."

My counselor, Paula, was one of a handful of amazing women who had taken me under their wing over the years. I was perceived as a misguided, wild young girl who needed a positive female figure in her life. These women probably saved me from some of the enduring pain that came from losing my mom. For months after she died, our neighbor Sandy Fosnaugh let me hang out with her and her family. I used to just walk into her house without knocking, until one day Sandy kindly told me that I better knock first and let someone answer the door. I felt that much at home there, and I'll never forget her admonishment.

For years after Mom was gone, Ethel, a married lady who lived around the corner, took me to drive-in movies and treated me to dinner once a month. I remember watching the new James Bond movie, *Live and Let Die*, in her cool house, decorated in feng shui flair. She said her Buddhas were good luck and a source of positive energy. I had loved spending time with her.

Mark's mom always opened the door to me, and Veronica watched out for me when I really needed someone. I feel indebted to these women who were all invaluable role models.

Leora was another amazing woman who came into my life. She was energetic, around thirty; she moved and talked nonstop about the meals she planned and the tent they had for me if I didn't want to sleep in the camper. She talked about the towns we'd drive through and how much she loved Owens Valley.

Her condominium was nothing short of beautiful. Leora had decadent leather furniture, plush carpet, an elaborate Sony stereo system, a spacious kitchen with sprawling counter tops, and a balcony with a view of the city. Leora was a registered nurse, but I had no idea what a nice place she had, or that she drove a Mercedes Benz convertible. I had no idea a nursing degree could be so lucrative.

Reiny looked around the room and picked up on my envy.

"Nurses don't do too bad. It's a worthwhile occupation, Tracy. Leora has helped a lot of people with their career. Just some food for thought."

Is Reiny encouraging me to go into the nursing field? He may have been my friend's uncle, but he seemed to care about me, as if he knew I was drifting and needed some help. The thought of becoming a nurse had never crossed my mind.

When Leora came back into the kitchen, Reiny wrapped his arms around her in a big hug. They were amazingly cute. From the beginning, it was fun to be around them, and I was glad I decided to go on the trip.

We loaded up Reiny's big plush camper and got my motorcycle onto the trailer with his other motorbikes. I offered to pay for the gas because I didn't want to be a freeloader, but Reiny wouldn't hear it. Before I knew it, we were churning down the road headed for one of the greatest trips I'd ever have in my life.

Dad would have never gone on a trip like Owens River. He was a city dweller through and through and had probably never considered a camping trip in his entire parenting life. In that respect, we were different; I loved camping.

It was a four-hour drive, and I had the entire camper to myself. I opened the curtains and watched the sights go by—Red Rocks, Lancaster, and Mojave. We paralleled the California aqueduct, which is also called the LA River when it reaches Los Angeles. I learned all sorts of things on that trip.

When we reached Owens Valley, Reiny pulled off the road in the middle of nowhere. A hot wind blew across the dry arid valley and the sun was high. Reiny pointed out Mount Whitney to the west and the Sierra Nevada mountains to the east, near Death Valley National Park. We crossed the road and saw a large wooden sign that said *Manzanar.*

Reiny explained how the government had relocated Japanese Americans to internment camps after the attack on Pearl Harbor. One of them was called Manzanar, where thousands were forced to live in makeshift housing, leaving behind all their belongings to be pillaged by their neighbors. I never learned about this in all my years of school.

By late afternoon, we pitched camp in a grassy field next to the river. Towering mountains surrounded us, and we saw dirt trails in every direction, a dirt bike riders paradise. The river was deep but fairly narrow and twisted and turned down the valley for more than a hundred miles. It was perfect for a casual float on our inner tubes, a perfect place to escape Dad and his wife.

Reiny's friends had teenagers my age, and for the next three days we camped, floated for miles on the lazy river, and rode our motorcycles whenever we wanted.

Even though I had been in two bad accidents, I never shook off my love for riding, despite breaking my leg and the accident with Tink. I struggled with the idea that I was responsible for his death, and often felt guilt and shame about it. Yet Tink's name never crossed my lips. I never told anyone about what had happened when I was age twelve because it still felt unimaginable and sounded too crazy. Still, it never stopped me from riding. I can't explain why. Maybe riding was in my blood. Or maybe I was just young and naive.

That weekend, I barely stayed off my Yamaha. I went all over the trails with my knobby tired motorcycle, climbing steep hills and going off jumps. I was getting pretty good, but one way or another, I always seemed to get hurt. The Owens River trip was no different. Luckily, it didn't turn out bad.

One evening, Reiny sent me to fetch the other kids for dinner. We could see them in the distance, riding around a jump track I must have been around fifty times myself. There were steaks, fresh potato salad, and corn on the cob ready to eat, and I was hungry. I jumped on my motorcycle, wearing just my shorts, a T-shirt, and my gym shoes. I never considered a helmet.

When I came to the jump track, I hit my rear brake hard to skid to a stop. My bare leg pressed into the hot exhaust pipe, burning a large area of my calf. I was in instant agony. Back at camp, I went straight to the river. The cool water was soothing, but the wound began to blister. Luckily, nurse Leora came to the rescue and insisted on dressing it up. She pulled out a tube of ointment, dabbed it on my red-hot wound, wrapped it in a gauze dressing and fetched some ice to put on it. I was fascinated by how she knew exactly what to do, as if it was instinctual.

"What kind of a nurse are you?"

Leora's eyes lit up.

"I've been teaching since 1973."

She taught psych nursing at LA County Mental Hospital, working with inmates near the USC campus. When she took the job, her supervisor asked if she understood that USC was in Watts, a tough area in LA. He was implying that it could be dangerous for a small White woman. She didn't care and took the job. I loved her open mindedness and her passion. I pictured her on a battlefield, like Florence Nightingale, who I read about in school. Leora seemed strong and capable, and I wanted to believe I was too, but becoming a nurse was another story.

I could only picture bedpans, blood, and sick old people. I didn't like any of those images. Blood wasn't so bad. It didn't make me queasy, but being a nurse meant being around sick people all the time and listening to their problems. I also flinched at the idea of working in a hospital where doctors barked orders and made nurses do their dirty work. I must have stored that idea in the back of my mind. Nursing was on my horizon, though, but I didn't know it yet.

I felt uneasy about going home. The thought of being around Dad and trying to get along with Gretchen felt strangely eerie and brought tears. It seemed like neither of them wanted me at the house. That made me sick to my stomach. Plus, I still hadn't heard anything from the Air Force and wondered if I was ever going to be accepted. If I didn't, I had no idea what I was going to do with my life. But connecting with people like Reiny and Leora made me hopeful.

43

Kicked Out

I felt it best to keep a low profile around the house. I wanted to avoid getting in anyone's way, making a mess, or annoying Gretchen. Despite my best effort, it wasn't going well. Gretchen became increasingly perturbed with my presence.

One time, I inadvertently parked my truck where she liked to park. When she got home, she vehemently insisted I move it immediately. When I played music by the pool it was always too loud. If I ate dinner with them, she'd talk about how hard she worked all day to help pay the bills, and then say how grateful I should be to have her cook me a hot meal. Her strict house rules were unpleasant, too. She closed all the windows while it was one hundred degrees outside and even hotter in the house. We had no air conditioning, but that didn't matter to Gretchen.

"There's a serial killer on the loose. He's killing people all across the valley. Keep the windows shut and the doors locked."

The killings had been all over the news. People were calling him another Walk-in Killer because he had raped and killed at least eight women in their homes. Gretchen was petrified.

"It's too hot to sleep with all the windows closed."

"I can't risk getting murdered in my sleep, Tracy."

I held back a chuckle. The odds of that happening were slim. She seemed irrational.

"Your Dad's going to dig out a little table fan for you."

I couldn't believe we were living in a hot stuffy house because of
a serial killer. Later, I convinced Gretchen that the windows in my
bedroom could be safely latched while partly open. It didn't help on
really hot summer nights, so I slept in the backyard on a pool raft.

While I tried to keep an open mind and be as cordial to Gretchen
as Dad would like, my patience ran thin. One night, I was on the
phone in the living room lounging with my feet on the coffee table
like I always had. Gretchen told me to move my feet and stood in the
archway, waiting for me to follow her orders. This table had been in
our house since I was a child when my mother was still alive. Why did
she care that my feet were on it? I didn't have my shoes on, just my
foam flip flops. *Is the table hers now?*

I wasn't sure what to do. Gretchen made me angry, staring at me
with her cocked hip and bossy tone. I decided not to budge and kept
my feet right where they were.

"The biggest problem I have is my dad's wife."

Gretchen glared. I could see her chest heaving. Before things got
out of hand, I thought it best to pull my feet off the table. Without
another word, Gretchen turned and walked away. I was certain she
was trying to drive me out of the house.

The next afternoon, I sat with Dad to watch *The Sands of Iwo
Jima.* He loved war movies and I always loved to watch them with
him. We'd watched dozens over the years. Gretchen was in the kitchen
making Dad a piece of toast just the way he liked. Nothing had been
said about the tiff we had in the living room. I couldn't tell if Gretchen
had told Dad. The bad vibe she had given off had subsided. She
seemed to be trying to be pleasant.

"Make a sandwich or something to eat if you'd like, Tracy."

She brought Dad a glass of milk and a piece of cake, and a little
later apple slices and decaffeinated coffee. It was nauseating how
much she doted over him. I wasn't about to compete with that even
if I wanted to, if that was what she was worried about. My goal was

to just get along as much as possible. By the end of the summer, I would be long gone.

A couple days later, I stopped and spoke with Dad while he worked on the van. By this time, it had evolved into more of a spectacle than I ever imagined. According to Dad, it had more than seven thousand silver dollars and Susan B. Anthony coins riveted onto it. Did Gretchen know that? There were so many it would be hard to count. There were ornaments everywhere, too, including a shining Pegasus on the hood as well as brass knives and swords. The dagger shapes scared me. What if he clipped a pedestrian? Impalement seemed likely.

"The van's looking good, Dad."

"I want to talk to you."

He picked up a brass toilet shaped piece and set it on a chunk of wood.

"Sure, what's going on?"

"It's about you living here."

"Yeah?" I swallowed.

"I'm not sure it's a good idea."

"It's Gretchen, right?"

Dad seemed annoyed. "She's doing everything she can to get along."

Dad explained how he didn't want anything screwing up his new marriage. He already had one dead wife, an annulment, and endless dead-end relationships. Gretchen was the woman he wanted to grow old with.

"It would be best if you moved out."

He picked up the hand drill and bore two holes in the toilet seat.

Ouch! "Wow. I didn't know it was that bad."

I was stunned. I felt instantly weary and sad and disappointed in Dad. He was kicking me out of his house. I felt my throat close up like a melon was lodged in there and tears well. I didn't want to cry. I told myself it would be a relief not to be there anymore. But it sure stung to think I was no longer welcome in my own father's house, my childhood home.

There was something twisted about it, yet it was a natural chain of events, straight out of a movie—middle-aged widower marries middle-aged woman; new wife turns into evil stepmother; grown teenager is no longer welcome. I should have seen it coming.

"I'll figure something out."

I swallowed, hiding from Dad how bad he made me feel. All my life I felt like I protected him from the bad feelings he caused. Somehow, I never wanted to make him feel bad from anything I did, but that left me vulnerable.

He finished drilling, blew the brass dust off the toilet seat, and opened the front door to the van. He pulled his wallet out of the glove box and handed me fifty bucks.

"Don't spend it all in one place."

I went straight to Santoro's Submarine Sandwich to get the best sub in the world. What was better to soothe a fresh wound? Santoro's had been serving subs in Burbank since 1956 and everyone knew it was the best. My longtime friend Ellen knew this too because she was there with her mom, Thelma, sharing a foot-long pastrami. They both looked happy to see me.

"Get a sandwich and come sit down with us."

When Ellen and I were in ninth grade, she threw a party at her house. Unlike Dad, Thelma was strict. She would stick around to chaperone. The place was full of young teeny boppers talking, listening to music, and figuring out a way to sneak rum into our Coca Cola. I had so much Bacardi in my Coke, I could hardly drink it. But Ellen's mom was no fool. She knew just by the way I sipped it that there was more in my drink than just soda.

"What you got in there?"

"Just some soda."

"No one sips soda like that."

I was tongue-tied, afraid she would smell my drink or take a sip and catch me red-handed. But Thelma let me off the hook and walked away to talk to Ellen.

Now, Ellen told me she moved to Colorado and happened to be visiting Burbank. Her boyfriend was a dentist and she worked in the same office as a hygienist in Estes Park. Ellen's brother, John, lived there as well, working as a realtor. When we were kids, John was a sheriff deputy until he was shot in the face and blinded in one eye. He received a huge settlement from the government and used some of the money to buy Ellen a brand-new Chevy Camaro. She had always been close to her big brother.

"How's your dad, Tracy? We saw him in his van down Hollywood Way the other day."

"He married Debbie Martin's mom."

I thought about Dad telling me I couldn't live at the house anymore. I didn't want to tell them about that. Instead, I talked about going to college with Mark and how I was now between career paths.

"I'm considering the Air Force."

Thelma gave me a surprised look.

"Really? The Air Force?"

She sounded like she didn't approve, and then explained how she was moving to Colorado, too.

"You should come out, Tracy. It's beautiful there. You and Ellen could share a place. She needs a roommate."

"Yeah, you should, Tracy. You would love it there. It's a cute little town with all sorts of shops and places you can work. Have you done any retail?"

The invitation to Colorado had possibilities. I could rent a place with Ellen and get a job. Staying in Burbank meant waiting indefinitely on the Air Force without a good place to live. I could probably stay with Steve and Allison, but that meant sleeping on their couch, which sounded like something close to hell. Going to Colorado could be my answer to getting out of Burbank again and getting away from Dad and his precious wife.

44

Greyhound to Denver

A month later, I was on a Greyhound bus to Denver. I left my Yamaha in Dad's backyard and sold my truck to a neighbor who gave me half of what I paid. I remember thinking I wouldn't need a truck in Estes Park. Ellen told me everything was within walking distance, and if I ended up joining the Air Force, I wouldn't need a truck, anyway.

When Ellen picked me up, we hugged excitedly. We loaded my three suitcases and Panasonic boombox into her Camaro and drove an hour to the cottage Ellen had rented. The little two bedroom sat on a ridge off a side road that felt like you were in a mountain forest. Smoke bellowed from a couple of chimneys in the neighborhood, which made me think of Camp Earl-Anna. I could only hope Estes Park would be as wonderful.

Estes Park was a cute little mountain town on the front range of the Rocky Mountains. It had a main street with little boutiques, coffee shops and seasonal festivities. Sometimes, I'd see more elk and moose wandering the streets than people. The beauty of the place blew my mind.

But from the start, I was miserable. Ellen spent most of her time working or going out with her boyfriend while I hardly knew anyone. I was too young to go to the local pubs. Ellen helped get me a job at the local pewter factory that was a short walk from our cottage. I had a brief interview and was hired on the spot for six dollars an hour. The factory was the largest building in town with more than one hundred people casting and designing molds and operating metal processing machines and kilns.

My job was the lowest on the totem pole—a pee wee mold shaver. I spent my entire shift sitting in front of an enclosed glass cubicle with my hands inside, shaving remnants of pewter off figurine molds. Hour after hour I buzzed molds of miniature animals, little people, inanimate objects, anything you could imagine.

It wasn't my idea of a good time. Once I had one pile of figurines shaved, someone came around and dumped in another load. There was never an end in sight. It was the most depressing job in the world. Sometimes, certain pieces of pewter reminded me of the brass on Dad's van. I decided I liked brass better.

The work was completely mindless. To help pass the time I listened to music on my Walkman. But music could only do so much. *How in the world am I going to do this eight hours a day?*

Jobs were posted for workers and others to apply, like shaving larger pewter pieces, operating casting machines, or more technical positions, like mixing the pewter alloy. That sounded the most interesting. The metals were locally mined, and pewter was a composition of lead, tin, and antimony. It made me wonder how brass was made. But for the three weeks I was there, I never got an opportunity for another job.

Meanwhile, Ellen was doing great. She had a job she liked. She and her dentist boyfriend were as happy as pie, and she seemed like she had her act together. I still hadn't heard from the Air Force and was feeling lonely. *What in God's name am I doing in Estes Park?*

I tried to venture out into town to explore. One afternoon on a beautiful autumn day, I went to Ellen's office to meet her after work and go to her friend's diner to get a bite. The Estes Park Hospital was kitty corner to her building, and as I waited for Ellen, I watched doctors, nurses, and ambulances come and go. I got to thinking about Leora and what she had told me about nursing. I had no idea what to do for a career. I knew what I didn't want to do but the question lingered; what should I be?

Becoming a nurse now seemed like a clear-cut goal as I increasingly liked the idea of helping people and learning the science of the human body. If I had a nursing degree, I could get a job as a registered nurse, an official RN. Nurses can get jobs all over the country, even across the world. College of the Redwoods had a nursing program.

The longer I sat there thinking about it the more excited I got. I would return to Eureka and get a nursing degree. That was the answer. It was a spontaneous decision that uplifted me. Just like that, I had a new plan for my life. I would have to apply for admission to nursing school at Redwoods, but I was confident I would get in if I took a few requisite classes and did well.

"Ellen, I'm going back to College of the Redwoods to get a nursing degree."

She looked stunned.

"But I just leased the cottage."

"I'm so sorry Ellen. I can't stay here."

"Well, that puts me in a bind, Tracy. I can't afford that place on my own."

"Is there someone else who would want the room?"

"Don't worry about it. I will figure it out."

I knew that Ellen felt like I was screwing her, because I was. But we left it at that. When I called Dad and told him what I was going to do, he liked the plan.

"I never thought the Air Force was for you."

He suggested that I come home, fetch the Riviera, and take it up north. The car had been unused and sitting parked on the street. Dad had to move it for the street cleaners. I would be doing him a favor by taking it, and I didn't have anything else.

45

The Worst Christmas Ever

Most of my dog-bite money was gone by the time I returned to College of the Redwoods. I had to depend on outside financial help and, luckily, I still had a Pell grant to pay tuition. What saved me was the Social Security check I got every month since Mom died, which wouldn't stop until I was twenty-three as long as I attended college. Mark's brother let me live in a trailer he had leased in Fortuna before returning to Burbank. He had paid the rent in full until June, so I could stay there for free.

Moving back to college happened in a hurry. I left Estes Park for Burbank. Without a good place to stay, I packed up the Riviera as fast as possible and headed north. That meant missing the holidays at home, but that's how it had to be.

It must have been my most miserable Christmas season ever if I don't count the first few after Mom died. I felt lonely and rejected by my dad. I was bummed with myself for ditching Ellen and quitting the pewter factory so abruptly, but sometimes a girl's gotta do what she's gotta do.

The dreary Humboldt weather didn't help, but the real problem was being alone. Mark had moved. Robert and Richard, who I still considered friends, were on holiday with their parents in Nigeria, and Beth was spending the holidays with her family. I was about to spend Christmas by myself, and I hated being alone.

Luckily, on Christmas Eve, I bumped into an old classmate who invited me over for dinner at her boyfriend's place. Being alone had made me feel like something was wrong with me. I missed my friends and having someone around who cared about me.

I was happy when winter classes finally began; I registered for a full load of classes, including biology, interpersonal communication, and technical writing. If I got those classes out of the way, I could get to the nursing prerequisites in spring and hopefully be accepted into the program the following fall. It was a heavy load, but the material was interesting, and I planned to work harder than ever to get my nursing degree. It was the clearest goal I'd ever had.

A month later, I ran into a junior high school friend. Glen worked at a gas station in Fortuna and shared an apartment with Alex, another old schoolmate of ours. They both went to my college and became born again Christians. Glen proselytized, telling me I should become a Christian because Jesus was the greatest person you could ever know. He explained how we all serve somebody, either the devil or the Lord, and that I had to make a choice. This was the time when Bob Dylan became a born again Christian and won a Grammy for his song, "Gotta Serve Somebody." Dylan became every Christians new hero.

I admit I was curious about all the Jesus talk. The idea of having a savior in my life was appealing, especially if knowing Jesus was anything like what Glen told me. For as long as I could remember, I thought that I was evil and destined for Hell because of all the bad things I had done. That's if in fact there *was* a Hell, and I had my doubts. According to the gospel, however, there was still hope for me. All I had to do was accept Jesus in my heart.

Since I was living alone in that little trailer, I'd become increasingly lonely, and my self-esteem once again crashed. When I wasn't in school, I was doing schoolwork. I hardly talked to my family. I partied with Beth from time to time, but I felt pretty alone in the world and life didn't have much meaning. Obtaining a nursing degree didn't feel tangible yet.

Glen could tell I was a ripe target. He got so excited about the prospect of converting me that he got one of his Christian friends on the phone to take a shot. Glen told me Lewis was a thirty-year-old Black man who had moved to Eureka from New York City.

"You're gonna love this guy."

When I heard his voice, he didn't sound aged thirty, or what I imagined a Black person would sound like, or like someone from the East Coast, but what did I know? I hadn't been around many Black people in my life. I realized I had some stereotypes that just weren't right. Lewis would go on to become one of my closest friends and trusted advisers. I felt fortunate to become his friend. Lewis was a real talker, different from anyone I had ever met. He was funny, smart, and I had a great time talking to him. He told me off-the-wall things about living in the Bronx, about going to a dentist who worked out of a garage, and how his father had beaten him with a belt if he didn't do his homework. Lewis wanted to know where I grew up and what my parents were like. I bragged about Dad's van and his eccentricity. We must have talked for an hour while Glen went outside and pumped gas.

It wasn't until the end of the conversation that we got to religion. Lewis loved the idea that my family was Jewish, and he couldn't believe I had never been to a synagogue or church. I was fascinated with the Scriptures he quoted, like "when two or three are gathered in His name, there the Holy Spirit dwells." The only thing I had known that was close to religion was all those names of books in the Bible that Mark's sister had made us memorize years before. I remembered most of them, but I didn't know anything about Jesus or what those books said about him. Lewis talked about how God is forgiving and knows everything about me, even the number of hairs on my head. I had my doubts that God would care about such trivia. *Doesn't God have more important things to think about?* But Lewis was sincere and not preachy, and many of the things he said rang true. I was starting to think there was something to this Christianity thing.

When I hung up, Glen was under the hood of some jalopy, checking the oil.

"I have to ask you something, Glen."

He wiped the dip stick with a rag. "Shoot."

"Do you have to go to church to be a Christian? Because church sounds boring."

"We can go somewhere where it's not boring at all."

"Oh yeah? Where's that?"

"I'll pick you up on Thursday night."

46

Born Again on the Lighthouse Ranch

G len drove an old Chevy van that had surfer stickers around the bumper; his surfboard was on the floor in the back. We headed to a place called the Lighthouse Ranch that was on Table Bluff overlooking the Pacific Ocean. It was like a camp, Glen said, where a bunch of Christians had turned an abandoned Coast Guard station into a commune. We were going to the weekly family night worship meeting.

Inside a large, two-story building we came to the mess hall where acoustic guitar music played a rhythmic folk-rock sort of tune. I sat down in the back with Glen, gawking at people singing, kneeling, and raising their hands in praise to Jesus. I'd never seen people act the way those Ranch people had. I couldn't get over their enthusiasm.

When the meeting ended, a tall bulky man with brown droopy eyes smiled at me.

"Now this must be Tracy."

Lewis took my hand and delicately shook it. He didn't live at the Ranch. He was visiting for family night, like Glenn and me. By the end of the night, I must have talked to a dozen people who were so friendly and interested in me that I felt instantly welcome. It was like nothing I'd ever experienced; after Dad and Gretchen wanted me gone, I longed for a place like the Lighthouse Ranch.

I kept attending there with Glen on Thursday nights and on weekends. After school, it became my favorite place. The setting was majestic, propped up on a high cliff with spectacular views of the ocean and the beautiful Eel River Valley, with miles of dunes and beaches.

I became friends with single people and married couples. Everyone was called brother and sister. Many were young, either passing through or looking for spiritual direction with other Christians. It had started back in the early '70's as part of the Christian movement, made up mostly of counterculture hippies who had given up drugs and converted. People who stayed had to be drug-free and willing to work.

Because the Ranch grounds were originally a Coast Guard training station, the complex had three houses to accommodate families who lived there. The main building above the kitchen and mess hall, housed dozens of newly married couples. The women's dorm house was strategically placed on the north end of the land, and the men's dorm was on the far south end where the Coast Guard once housed their recruits. There were around one hundred people living out at the Ranch at the time.

Sometimes a bunch of us loaded into Glen's van to go to the beach on weekends. If the waves and wind were just right, Glen put on his wetsuit and surfed. Glenn's roommate, Alex, took some of us to the dunes to go four-wheeling. We bounced around together, and I laughed so hard my stomach hurt.

One night, Glenn and Alex hosted us, and after dinner we sat around their living room for Bible study, specifically the beatitudes in the Book of Matthew. Glen handed me an open Bible with red lettering inside. The red words depicted the actual words of Jesus.

"Blessed are the meek, the merciful, the peacemakers."

It was like a behavioral life lesson, and the words lit us up with joy and hope. My new friends talked about what being a Christian meant to them. They all seemed so happy and content with their choice to follow Jesus, the man born of a woman and incarnated to be the savior of the world. In the Bible, he sounded like an amazing person who healed people, accepted them, and sacrificed his life for them. When he rose from the dead through the power of God, it was either a huge elaborate scheme, or he really was the savior of the world. I wanted to believe the latter.

Before long, I thought I had to make a choice. If I was going to spend time with these Christians and buy into their way of life, I should probably accept Jesus into my heart. I was in a bit of a dilemma because I liked the freedom to drink beer and smoke pot. But I had resolved that doing those things wasn't going to work with Jesus and this group of Christians, who believed that drinking and smoking were not righteous. To them, it was a sin and a knock on a person's character to indulge in drugs and alcohol.

Oh, what the hell!

I decided one day to accept Jesus and become a follower. I wanted to be a part of this. I went back to my trailer, got down on my knees, and repented for my sins as I was told to do, and I asked Jesus to take me in.

I was now born again.

After I got baptized by Lewis and Glen at an informal ceremony in the school pool, I went to microbiology class and told the two people sitting next to me what I had just done. They looked at me similarly to the way people looked at Dad walking around in his Speedos. But I was proud and excited about my decision. I felt like telling the whole world.

Still, I knew school had to be my focus. More than anything, I wanted my nursing degree. It took me three semesters to get all the prerequisites I needed. I had good grades in microbiology, anatomy and physiology, and organic chemistry. I applied in the winter of 1984 and found out a month later that I'd been accepted into the nursing program. I would start in autumn. I'd never been so proud of myself.

With a few months free before school started, I moved to the Lighthouse Ranch. There was space for me in the single women's house and I thought it would be fun. I loved the idea of spending more time with some of the friends I'd made there.

The Christian fellowship was by far my favorite part. Every Sunday, dozens of us took the Ranch bus to town for church at Gospel Outreach, which owned and oversaw the Ranch. The town folks and church leaders were just as kind and friendly as the people at the Ranch, and I made lots of friends there, too.

On the Ranch, we all had to work, making meals, or doing odd jobs assigned to us. Sometimes I was told to do phone soliciting for one of the businesses the Ranch owned. When I first moved in, I was told to turn in an application at a local daffodil farm. For a week, I picked them in the pouring rain with mud up to my knees. I'd never worked so hard in my life.

At the end of the week, we turned our paychecks over to the Ranch leaders. I didn't mind. I was given a bed and hot meals, and I didn't need much money. I was still collecting Social Security, saving most of it for when school started. I always had a little spending money, but I didn't dare breathe a word of that to the Ranch leadership. They'd probably want me to turn the check over to them. I would use that money for my schooling, so I didn't worry about it.

I called Dad every once in a while from the Ranch. He always had a new story to tell about how he and Gretchen were drawing crowds at Venice Beach or somewhere in Vegas. I didn't explain my religious conversion or that I was living in a Christian commune. It wasn't that he would disapprove or question my choices. He had a way of staying neutral on big life decisions. I figured I would share it with him someday face-to-face, maybe even get him to consider Jesus and become born again.

Toward the end of summer Steve called. He must have gotten the number from Dad. Steve was on a road trip with his new girlfriend and wanted to visit. He showed up a couple hours later and we walked to the edge of the bluff, where a big wooden cross stood. I talked a little about becoming a Christian, and how good life was with my brothers and sisters and the Lord. Steve and his girlfriend looked at me like I was crazy. When we walked by a group of brothers holding Bibles, Steve wrapped his arm around me.

"Tracy, is this some kind of cult?"

His girlfriend, Lisa, laughed out loud like it was really funny. I didn't like that. I thought she was a bit skanky. She had long clumpy hair, thick eyebrows, and wore short cut-offs and a revealing tight tank top. She was the exact opposite of Steve's longest and sweetest girlfriend who was also named Lisa.

"It's not a cult, Steve. And I'm starting nursing school in September."

His comment got me thinking. *Am I in a cult?* The Ranch made me feel welcomed and part of something larger, but I wasn't the kind of person who would fall prey to a cult. I was there of my own free will. I had always struggled with authority. If anyone tried to tell me what to do or demanded things I didn't feel comfortable with, I'd be out of there.

For the most part, I liked the leadership of three young married couples. Some had lived on the Ranch for years. They oversaw the drudgery of the work that was required to keep the place running, from managing the small businesses the Ranch owned, to managing the personalities and drifters who showed up.

The Ranch gave most anyone a meal and a place to sleep for the night. Those who decided to stay had to work and follow the rules. If not, they made you leave.

I was ripe and ready to be a functional member of the community, and I was interested in learning more about the Bible. I also felt I could come and go pretty much any time I wanted. The leadership wasn't strict with curfews. I still had my Riviera and would drive some of us into town for ice cream, or down to the jetty, or up the canyon for warm days on the river.

We got pretty wild in the sister's house, too. We were all young and full of energy. We'd stay up late watching movies, talking, telling stories, and laughing in our living room. Brothers came over sometimes to visit, but the leaders were weird about intermingling with the opposite sex.

"Avoid the appearance of evil."

That was a common phrase, and fooling around would get you kicked out for sure.

The leaders came down on people from time to time for not performing assigned tasks. At least once a week, I'd see one person called in for a meeting about their behavior.

One day, I saw one of my dorm sisters visibly upset. Alice was one of the sweetest and caring people in the whole house. We worked together phone soliciting until she became the Ranch shopper, responsible for buying everything from food to toilet paper. She wanted to move into town to live with a friend. When the Ranch leaders heard of her plans, they called her in for a meeting and counseled her not to leave, saying that she wasn't ready to go into the world. Alice was heartbroken. She didn't want to go against the counsel of her elders, but she wanted a change. Something about the whole thing made my blood boil. *Are the leaders on some power trip?* I'd heard of them doing things like this to several Ranch residents. I didn't know the details of Alice's situation, but it seemed manipulative. I became skeptical.

Six months after I moved to the Ranch, I was called in. Cher, who was just a little older than me, told me how the Ranch was for people in certain walks of life and that I wasn't getting what they intended for me. She was probably right. I had developed a cavalier attitude when it came to Christianity. I found parts of the Bible intriguing and helpful, but I often didn't participate in religious discussions. I was still nineteen and didn't like the seriousness that being religious seemed to require. I got bored. I mostly liked talking and laughing with the others or going on outings and having fun.

"We have enjoyed having you here."

I was a bit confused.

"Are you telling me I have to leave?"

They shared glances and nodded in unison.

"You know, I was planning to leave at the end of the month?"

"It's best if you went sooner. We have a girl coming in from Sacramento and it would be nice to move her in with Sharon and Treena, since you were going anyway."

They wanted me out by Sunday.

Getting kicked out bothered the shit out of me. I hadn't broken any rules, behaved poorly, or used illicit drugs. I hadn't smoked pot since the day I accepted Jesus. It felt hurtful like when Dad wanted me out of his house. I guess I was having too much fun, and the leaders didn't like it. Maybe they felt I was taking advantage of the Lighthouse Ranch. Maybe I was. But it was sure fun while it lasted.

47

My Friend Lewis

I was lucky to have left the Ranch when I did. There was a room available in one of the big houses the Gospel Outreach church owned in town. My great new friend Lewis lived there and helped me get a place in the huge, four-story Victorian they called H Street House.

It was always alive with the hustle and bustle of a dozen people coming and going, and I thrived in that environment. Aside from sharing one bathroom with eleven others, I loved living there, and rent was just two hundred a month.

The H Street House was church affiliated and more or less a religious communal house, which meant church people popped over all the time to hang out. On Tuesday nights, an elder hosted his home church group in the living room.

Everyone was expected to be devoted to God and act appropriately. You couldn't get away with boozing it up or lighting a joint, but my roommates were incredibly nice and fun, and head over heels about Jesus. I liked gathering in Lewis's room to hang out and talk about our jobs or schoolwork, church politics, relationships, and how Jesus fit into all of it.

Lewis was completely different from anyone I ever knew. He was witty and insightful and had a pastoral way about him. Having him in the house was like having our own private guru. Everyone flocked to him for his funny sense of humor and his insights that often proved true. He noticed everything—if you were depressed or unusually happy, or if you were frazzled from school or a day on the job. He listened and asked all the right questions. He wasn't afraid to tell the truth about what he thought of you, and his advice was usually quite helpful.

Lewis knew people at the Ranch, church leaders, and families all around Eureka. He was always visiting people, and he started bringing me along. We went to the Omey's house for Christmas Eve dinner, and the Moores' after Sunday church for brunch. I got to know two women high up in leadership at a sisters' retreat, and the three of us became good friends.

With a lot of help from Lewis, I built a real home and was part of a great community. Dad and Burbank felt more distant than ever, and it was about to get even more so.

By spring of that year, things became strange at the church. A division erupted among leadership for reasons I didn't fully understand. The people I liked and admired wanted to go in a more charismatic direction, focusing on the gifts of the Spirit, like prayer for healing and the power of prophecy, while the main leaders were wary of that direction.

I didn't have a strong opinion either way. I liked it the way it was, but I didn't see anything wrong with trying new things. Either way, it was heartbreaking to hear that a bunch of my friends were leaving the church.

Lewis had connected me with Steve and Layne Fish, a leadership couple. They were in their mid-thirties; They had met at the Lighthouse Ranch when they were hippies back in the '70's. Over the last ten years, they had ascended into important roles within the church. They invited me for dinner and told me about their lives and what the Ranch was like when they had lived there. They had five young kids that I babysat a couple times.

Layne Fish loved to talk about the Scriptures, and she and I spent a few sessions going through them. She was a great spiritual teacher and always seemed sincere when she talked about Jesus. I looked up to her. I trusted them and they seemed to trust me. When they left, I wanted to go, too. They were moving to the Pacific Northwest and said I could stay with them up in Washington state if I was interested in moving up that way.

I took the offer seriously. I liked the idea of being a part of their family. It was the sort of structure that had been sorely lacking in my own upbringing. Mom dying had thrown a wrench into how our family was supposed to be. Then Dad, in some ways going off the deep end, left the rest of us flailing in every direction. I was hungry for the normalcy of the Fish family; it was something I had longed for all my life. Between the Ranch telling me to leave and the weird church split, I was ready to move on. I was ready for a new adventure.

As my first year of nursing school came to an end, I asked Steve Fish if the offer was still open. He told me there was a spare bedroom in their house, and he thought the rent for room and board would be a good deal for all of us. I'd also found out my credits from College of the Redwoods would transfer to Clark College, the nursing school I would be attending in Washington state.

I sold the Riviera, which was falling apart, and bought a Ford Fiesta, a dependable car that could get me around for half the cost. My H Street roommates were excited for me and gave their blessings. By late June, I was on the road north, headed to a new adventure.

48

Riding with Ray

With my Fiesta packed to the gills, I took the coastal highway north through Crescent City, where humongous old growth redwoods shadowed the oceanfront. The highway veered east through more forests and eventually north to the Oregon border. When I hit Interstate 5, I thought of Dad. In Burbank, the same interstate was called the Golden State Freeway. Dad used it all the time, and I pictured him making his way to the vacuum store.

With the increasing miles between us, I felt a softening in my heart for my dad. I missed him. I missed his fun-loving spirit and the brightness in his eyes when he looked at me. He had no idea how to raise me, but he loved me with all he had. He must have done something right. I wasn't doing too badly; I had to give him some of the credit for that.

I settled into my basement bedroom at the Fish's house, and enrolled in my courses at Clark College in Vancouver, Washington. I was frustrated that I needed an extra chemistry course and another writing class to transfer into their nursing school. My government grants didn't cover as much tuition as they did in-state in California, so my finances were borderline. I got a part-time job through a nursing agency as a certified nursing assistant. I traveled around the Portland area, caring for old people in convalescent hospitals. It was grueling at times, but it sure helped pay my bills.

I spent lots of time with the Fish family, hanging out with their kids and going to church, which was small and intimate and gave me an instant good vibe. The worship band played good music for praise, and most everyone seemed kind and sincere. I felt entirely at home there. I made my first friend in Sharon Buckley, a California girl who worked for the Air Force Reserves and dreamed of being a missionary.

A week before Christmas, Sharon introduced me to a dark-haired fellow, six feet tall with straight white teeth, holding a motorcycle helmet. His name was Ray Bouvier, and the minute I heard him talk about his Yamaha Heritage Special, I had an instant crush.

"I haven't had the bike long, but I love it."

He was easily one of the most appealing guys I'd met in a long time. I wanted him to take notice of me.

"I used to ride. My whole family rides."

I exaggerated, but he nodded and seemed impressed.

"That's great."

"Can I ride it?"

I couldn't help making a spectacle of myself. At first, I thought Ray was surprised at the question, but then he looked out the window.

"It's dark out. You want to ride it now?"

"Yeah, maybe not. Daytime would be better."

"How about tomorrow?"

The following day, we met during his lunch hour in downtown Portland. We took a ride up in the hills above the city. I handled the motorcycle like I knew I would. Since I still didn't have a motorcycle license, Ray took over after a few miles. I enjoyed straddling the bike behind him, and I made a point to hold on tight to his waist.

We exchanged phone numbers and started talking incessantly on the phone in the evenings. Ray lived across the river in Beaverton, Oregon, so the calls were considered long distance back then, even though we were only fifteen miles apart. That didn't stop us. The coolest part was how easy this guy was to talk to.

Ray was raised mostly in Oregon. His dad was an IRS agent who had moved his family around a lot when Ray was growing up. Even so, Ray enjoyed a pretty stable childhood all the way to college. Then his mom left his dad for a mailman she worked with at the post office. Once Ray graduated from college, he lived with his dad until he got his first job as an actuary and moved into his own apartment.

Ray was confident and smart, and he had been much more sheltered than me. I think our very different upbringings and perspectives were part of the attraction. We found each other interesting. I could tell we were forming a special connection, and it seemed clear he liked me more than I deserved.

On Christmas Eve, Ray got off work early and called. We were both bored. Ray was spending the evening with his dad, brother, and sister in-law, and asked if I wanted to come over. I was overjoyed. Ten minutes later, I was headed to Beaverton in the pouring rain.

I made it just before Ray's dad served up spiral ham sandwiches and mashed potatoes. Ray's dad was sweet, soft spoken and interesting. He talked about traveling through Europe and skiing on Mount Hood in Oregon with a new singles group he'd joined. He was the same height as my dad and seemed as normal as a dad could be. I wasn't looking for normal in Ray, but normal*ish* seemed like a good thing. Someone once told me, if the dad is a decent person then the son most likely will be, too. That made sense.

After peppermint ice cream, Ray surprised me with a gift wrapped in the Sunday funnies. I ripped the paper open after deciding not to worry that I didn't bring him anything. It was a crooked shaped coffee mug that said, *Nobody's Perfect*. I instantly loved it and thought it was a gutsy move to give to someone you didn't know that well. Ray knew I'd see it as a harmless joke and that was true. Nobody is perfect.

I thought this Ray was a real keeper.

We took off in my car to find a midnight snack. Lyon's, where Ray worked as a busboy in high school, was the only place open. We sat for hours, eating French fries, and talking about everything under the sun.

Over the next few months, I realized Ray was the greatest catch I'd ever landed. I hadn't been romantically interested in a guy since high school, but Ray had everything I found attractive. For starters, he was always on time, and never swore or raised his voice. He was incredibly smart and articulate. He had a good job as an actuary, a profession I knew nothing about even after he tried to explain it.

I was amazed by how much he knew about the Bible, and how he talked about it in such practical terms. For example, he hated racism and bigotry and pointed out how Jesus showed by example how to treat others. He compared prominent Christian leaders of today to the religious pharisees of Biblical times. Neither of us could stand televangelists. We knew they were frauds out for people's money.

Ray talked about the lies of the Vietnam war, the truth about the Iran Contra affair, and he liked Jimmy Carter and thought Ronald Reagan was bad for the country. I was apathetic about the two presidents and generally uninformed about politics. But the more Ray talked about things, the more interested I became. I started to pay more attention to world events and wanted to know facts and details so I could figure things out on my own. He liked that about me. He wanted me to think for myself. The more I was around Ray, the more self-confident and positive I became.

The experience was changing me mentally and physically. I started losing weight, which was unexplainable. I was eating half as much as I used to, and I seldom indulged in dessert. I didn't want it. My dietary moderation seemed out of character and started to concern me. At the time, I was studying the respiratory system. Tuberculosis lit up in my mind. *Could I have TB?* I had recently tested positive for the TB skin test that I needed for work, and I had chest X-rays to make sure my lungs were clear, which they were. But I still had some symptoms—weight loss, a recent fever, loss of appetite. I was concerned and told Layne Fish who exploded in laughter.

"You're sick in love Tracy."

She was right; Ray and I did everything together. When we weren't playing football in the field next to the church, or eating pizza and watching movies with friends, it was just Ray and I spending time together. When I wasn't studying, all I could think about was Ray from Oregon who rode a motorcycle and liked just about everything I liked. We talked about sports and played on a softball team together. We both loved music and grew up loving the same bands, like Pink Floyd and Queen. We spent our first official date at the Oregon Symphony Orchestra, conducted by the legendary James DePriest. I never had a friend I could share so much with, and I didn't want it to ever end.

When I told Ray my dad was eccentric, that he dyed his facial hair and wore a toupee, and decorated his van with trinkets and coins, Ray didn't seem to care.

"Well, it's good he's not boring."

49
A Visit Home

I called Dad to tell him about Ray and how serious things were getting between us.

"You should bring him down. I'd like to meet him."

The idea of Dad meeting Ray was daunting. I had told Ray very little about him and how much he stood out in a crowd. I completely downplayed the van and didn't even show him a picture. There was no telling how much Dad would embarrass me in front of Ray. There was no controlling him with his off-color jokes and childhood stories he'd tell about me. I didn't know if Dad would freak Ray out or not. But then again, I wanted Ray to know Dad and where I came from. I wanted him to see all of me. If he didn't, then what was the point? If my family turned out to be too much for Ray, I wanted to know now.

A month later, we were on a plane to Burbank. When we came out of the gate, Dad was waiting for us. I hadn't seen him in more than three years, but he looked and dressed like he always did—an unbuttoned blue dress shirt with a chest pocket, dark blue pants, and black leather shoes. The only thing new was his pierced left ear donning eight diamond studs.

"How's my girlies?"

Dad hugged me and kissed me on the lips. Then I introduced him to Ray.

"How you doing Ray?"

Dad reached out to shake hands, and Ray returned Dad's firm grip, "Nice to meet you, Ernie."

Dad told us how it took him a while at airport security because he had to take off his belt to get through the metal detector. Getting his silver dollar belt out of the loops of his pants was a big deal, and of course he had to show us the holographic eyeball on his belt buckle. It was big and colorful, and followed you when you moved.

"Look into my eyes."

Ray laughed and focused to get a better look.

"That's awesome, Ernie."

Dad went on about the time he was late for a flight in Hawaii. He had no time to take off his belt at security, so he took off his pants, belt buckle and all, and set them on the conveyor belt. I had never heard this story, and it was a doozie. He assured us he had his bathing suit underneath. Everybody stood slack jawed, staring, like he was an alien. The woman behind him gasped and turned away.

"I thought she was going to faint."

"Who could blame her, Dad? Your Speedo shows everything."

My face flushed when I looked at Ray. I had just pointed out Dad's bulging crotch. I walked right into that one. I chalked it up as my first embarrassment, one of many. Dad wasn't wasting any time.

Dad snatched my bag and we started for the exit. Ray squeezed my hand. He seemed happy and excited, and I could tell he was getting a kick out of Dad.

When we got outside, the first thing that caught my eye was my old friend, the van, glistening in the sunshine. It was parked at the curb, less than a hundred feet from the entrance. People were gathered around it, and I wished I had warned Ray. There must have been twice as many pieces riveted on the van from the last time I'd seen it.

I had this fear that Ray would think I was too strange and lose interest if he knew the extent of Dad's weirdness and the madness of his van. I prayed that it wasn't some big mistake bringing Ray home.

Two kids were on the curb playing with some of the brass bells and trinkets. The van was like an amusement park to small children. They stood up and watched our every move, the way kids do when someone does something they don't understand. The adults watched us, too, and didn't seem to care that they were staring.

The side door was so heavy now that Dad needed both arms to lift it onto the roller so it would slide open. I insisted Ray take the captain seat up front. I was happy to be behind the tinted windows, away from all the gawking eyes, wondering who the hell these people were. I was twenty-three and still embarrassed by my Dad. I didn't understand myself. *Why do I still care?*

A cop standing beside his motorcycle waved to Dad.

"Have a nice day, Ernie."

Dad told Ray how the airport police let him park in the red zone because he was a local celebrity. "They really just want a chance to get a closer look at my van."

I counted my blessings. I'd often worried about Dad and his van. A collision with the van would demolish any car with its massive weight and sharp protruding objects. If a pedestrian ever got in its way, they would surely be impaled. Dad would be sued to kingdom come.

Then there were the coins to consider. It would be easy to steal them. All you needed was a drill and a bit to ream out the rivets. Despite that, nothing had ever been stolen. What about the defacing of US currency? Dad had drilled holes in thousands of silver dollars and other coins. I thought that was a crime, and that the government cared about stuff like that. Thank God they didn't, at least not in Dad's case.

Gretchen made us dinner. She was as warm and loving as could be. Neither one of us held a grudge from what happened in the past. I realized I was a brat back then and knew the hostilities weren't entirely her fault. I wanted to let bygones be bygones.

She was in constant motion, setting the table, pouring us water, and clearing the dishes. When Ray offered to help, Gretchen insisted he sit, and Dad jumped right in.

"That there is one incredible woman."

"I'm sure she is, Ernie."

Dad regaled Ray with colorful stories about going to Las Vegas.

"A sheik once offered me a hundred grand for my van. I turned him down because I bet I could get more for it later."

Ray and I doubted that, but who knew?

Dad asked Ray what he did for a living and Ray explained that he was a pension plan consultant, basically a numbers cruncher who helped companies run their retirement funds. It was fantastic listening to two of my favorite humans learning about each other. I loved that Ray had a lucrative job, but it did sound boring. I could tell that Dad liked that Ray had a good paying job.

Ray quickly changed the subject.

"I saw you and the van on *Real People* a few years back."

Ray loved the fact that he had seen the van on TV long before he met me.

Dad bragged about his appearances on *The Will Shriner Show* and the van being used on *Arsenio Hall*. For some reason, he told the story of when I was a child and escaped down the street naked and how the police brought me back.

"This kid sure loved to run around naked."

"Nice story, Dad. Thanks a lot."

Ray chuckled and squeezed my thigh.

He loved Dad. He listened to his stories and loved that he constantly told jokes and seemed to enjoy life. Ray didn't mind that Dad often dominated the room and was constantly talking, mostly about himself. He could see that Dad was also thoughtful and kind and a really nice guy. By the end of the weekend, I was relieved that the visit went really well.

When it was time to leave, Dad took us to the airport and a security man let him park in the red zone. I could hardly believe it. Dad thanked the man through his window.

"Anytime, Ernie. Happy to see you."

We were fifty feet from the main entrance.

Dad insisted I take one of his Hoovers back with me.

"I can't have my kid borrowing a vacuum for God's sake."

Dad took apart a rebuilt Hoover so Ray and I could carry it on the plane. Of course, everyone who saw Dad walking through the terminal stopped to stare. This time, they watched him carry a vacuum motor like it was a briefcase. I didn't mind the stares anymore, as they came with the territory of having the eccentric Ernie Steingold as a parent. I had to admit, it was fun.

At the gate, Dad clutched my hand and pulled me in to peck me on the lips. He turned to Ray and shook his hand firmly.

"Take care of my girl."

Dad choked up. I gave him a one-armed hug, squeezed his waist, and rested my head on his shoulder. Saying goodbye was hard for me, too. When I turned to get a last glimpse, he waved. As I headed down the ramp, I hoped it wouldn't be too long before I saw my dear ol' dad again.

Dad and Gretchen. Ultimately, I thought they were good together.
They were happy and took care of each other. 1980's

Here's Mark Hillis and his dog Bo
in front of his pot plant. About
1982 in Fortuna California. I can't
find any pictures of us together.
We were always taking pictures
of each other.

From left to right: Me, Lewis, roomie Frank on the front porch of H Street House in Eureka, California. 1985

My dad liked to shake hands with people, both men and women. But he put an extra squeeze on the guys like here with Ray Bouvier, my husband to be. Burbank 1986

This is 1995 just before we moved to Burbank from Seattle. These were the greatest times, living near my dad again and spending so much time with him.

Those are my little tots. Julia the babe crying and Emily behind Dad's arm. The van could make some kids happy and curious. In this case not so much.

From the left: Me, my sister, Allison, and my brother Steve reunited after ten years. I treasure my beautiful siblings. I feel having them legitimizes me and the world I grew up in. 1998

Here's Dad on a typical Tuesday. Around 1996

Dad came up from Burbank to Portland Oregon to give me away.
June 1988

50
Time to Get Married

Much as I enjoyed living with the Fishes, I moved out before the start of my final year of nursing school. I needed to branch out on my own. Layne told me about an apartment overlooking the Columbia River that was a short drive away and within my budget.

To help offset the rent, the owner, Wes, a Seventh Day Adventist, hired me to help him plant trees on his land. They were large with big balls of roots about fifteen feet tall. We worked for weeks but never on Saturdays because his religion forbade working on the Sabbath, just like some Jews. A day of rest. No work at all. I thought that was weird. We could work on Sundays, my adopted Sabbath, which was ironic and made me think religion was full of nonsense.

Out my front door was a view of the river between tall deciduous trees whose leaves were starting to turn to fall colors. It was beautiful and seemed perfect, but soon after I moved in, I discovered again that I hated living alone. All I could do out there was homework and read or listen to the radio. I wasn't used to being alone. At school, I never wanted to go home. My friends never visited because I was far out of the way. When Ray came to see me, it was a long motorcycle ride across the city and over country roads.

Sharon, the girl at church who introduced me to Ray, saved me. She and I were two of only three young women in the church's singles group, and we had a blast together. Sharon was a fantastic friend, sweet and kind with a big smile and a contagious laugh. We would eventually share a two-bedroom apartment in southeast Portland, just a mile away from church and Ray. It was still a distant drive to campus, but my nursing hospital was close by.

In December, I got an offer I couldn't refuse; Ray wanted to marry me. This great guy, loving me the way he did, was the most grounding experience I've ever had. He knew a lot about the big stuff I went through as a kid, and he never judged me. I have nothing but love for this guy who made me feel ways I'd never felt before. Ray was it. We planned to marry in June 1988.

I delivered my graduating class benediction and Ray did the honors of pinning me with my nursing pin on stage before all my friends, in an auditorium full of about five hundred people. I couldn't believe that my class of twenty-eight nurses had so many people there to see us graduate. Dad couldn't be there, but he loved the idea of me becoming a nurse. Dad kept saying on the phone how proud of me he was.

I was flabbergasted when I was asked to deliver a speech. I had plenty of experience talking before small audiences in school, but on that day, I was pretty nervous. Ray coached me, reminding me to do things a good speaker does, like make eye contact with the audience and not to speak too fast. I thought I did pretty well, and I was proud of myself. It was a day I will never forget.

51
Family Reunion

It was time to get married. I had passed the state test and secured my nursing license, and I had time to invite everyone I knew that I could still contact. But what I cared about most was having my family there. My relationship with siblings Steve and Allison had grown distant over the years, but both were thrilled to come, and so was Dad. I was ecstatic.

Two days before the wedding, Dad and Gretchen flew in from Burbank. I met them in the lobby of the hotel I had recommended, a block from our church where we'd be married. It was the first time Dad had ever traveled to see me, and now he would be giving me away.

I had dressed up a little in a chiffon blouse, fitted jeans, cute hanging earrings and some makeup. I'd been trying to look my best since I started dating Ray. I had lost more weight and wanted to be more of a lady.

Dad noticed as he leaned in to kiss me.

"You look great."

It felt great to hear him say so. I had a lot of anxiety about the wedding and wanted everything to go well, and so far, I felt happy and loved by everyone.

Allison arrived later that day, my maid of honor. I loved my sister and recognized how much she had come through for me when we were kids. She carried a lot on her shoulders after Mom died. Dad had been incredibly hard on her, which damaged her. I'm not sure she'd admit that, but I think it's true. We all got damaged. But Allison was strong and capable.

She left behind her baby daughter and husband in California for our weekend festivities. Being my *matron* of honor, as she corrected me, was a responsibility she took seriously.

Steve, who I hadn't seen since that day at the Lighthouse Ranch, arrived with his fiancé, Cherie. His bride-to-be was my age, a Southern bell from Louisiana with a strong accent. I loved her right away. She had a fun sense of humor and was always cracking witty jokes. She was a real beauty, too, with long, natural blond hair and beautiful blue eyes. I couldn't help thinking that she looked like Mom when she was young in her flowery sundress. I rarely thought about my mother, but maybe Steve subconsciously saw her in Cherie.

Steve had been painting houses, airplanes, and oil rigs for a living. He met Cherie, who was a dental assistant, during a cleaning. It took four appointments to get my brother's teeth pristine because he hadn't been to a dentist in so long. Every time he came in, Cherie insisted on helping. She had an unrelenting crush on my big brother. Eventually, they got serious and moved to Cherie's hometown in Louisiana.

Being seven years apart, Steve and I were never super close. But I was excited that he wanted to travel across the country and be part of my wedding. We were bound to get closer because of it, and Steve stood by Ray for all the wedding preparations.

The next morning, while Dad and Gretchen explored the city, Ray and I met with Allison, Steve, and Cherie to decorate the church. I would have preferred a more formal setting with classic architecture and stained-glass windows, but the place was free, thanks to our pastor who also married us. I couldn't complain and even felt lucky.

We used streamers, bells, and helium balloons to make the place look festive, along with bouquets of carnations. I thought the decor was a mix of cheesy and classy, making for a laid-back atmosphere.

We were being economical so Ray and I would have money for a honeymoon.

Allison had plans for the rest of our day.

"I was thinking me and Cherie would take little sister here out for lunch. Girls only. You guys can go get a burger or something, and we'll meet you back here in a couple hours."

Allison didn't have a clear plan, but she seemed open to just about anything.

"It's such a nice day. We should do something outside. Is there any horseback riding around here?"

Allison was a horseback-riding fanatic, and hitting the trails around the Pickwick stables in Burbank had probably been her favorite childhood pastime. I knew a place in a rural area in the middle of Portland. It was only a mile from where we were. The day was warm, and the sky was blue, perfect for an equestrian ride.

We took the side road along a creek and parked in front of the stable. A couple horses stood outside in the corral. Bugs buzzed and the smell of horses wafted through the open windows. Cherie hadn't been paying attention as we drove.

"A horse stable? You gotta be kidding. I'm wearing a miniskirt. I'm not riding a horse in a miniskirt."

Allison had to agree.

"Shit. I'm in my heels. I can't ride in these either."

I looked down at my feet.

"I'm wearing sandals."

We cracked up in tearful laughter and couldn't move for a while we were so much in stitches. It would have been great horseback riding with my big sister and Cherie on my last day as a single woman, but it wasn't in the cards. Allison had other ideas.

"Let's go get a Bloody Mary."

I had never been a big fan of that drink, and I rarely drank alcohol since I'd been going to church. I liked a beer once in a while, but just to be polite. I forced myself to drink two and had a bit of a buzz before Allison suggested we go to my apartment to look at my wedding dress.

"I heard your dad bought the dress for you, Tracy. That was sure nice of him."

"I ordered it out of the JC Penney's catalog."

Allison wasn't as impressed as Cherie.

"Hell, it's the least he could do. Dad went cheap the day he married Gretchen."

His only contribution to my wedding was buying my dress. It was the only thing I felt comfortable asking for. I'd been paying my own way for years, and between Uncle Sam, a student loan, and working part-time, I was getting by alright. Dad wanted to put his hard-earned money into the van or vacations with his wife. All three of us kids had learned to expect that. I was twenty-four already and didn't feel like Dad owed me anything.

At the apartment, Allison and Cherie watched me unzip the bag the dress was shipped in.

"You haven't taken it out of the bag?"

"I did when I first got it. I thought I should keep it in the bag to keep it clean."

"It's going to be wrinkled as all hell in that bag, Tracy. Let's have a look."

Allison placed the dress on my bed. It was wrinkled beyond belief. The buzz I had from the Bloody Mary's quickly dissipated. Allison looked at her watch.

"You got an iron? We got three hours until the wedding rehearsal."

The only appliance I had was the vacuum Dad had given me. But Sharon had an iron. She always ironed her clothes for work. I set up her ironing boarding board and Allison ironed away at the long, tulle silk dress, accented with lace and short beaded sleeves. For the eighty dollars Dad had paid, it really was beautiful.

As Allison ironed, it got hotter and hotter in the apartment.

"You got any beer in this place?"

"Sorry, no beer."

"Well, go to the store and get some. We're working our asses off here."

Allison was saving me. I hadn't even considered the dress getting wrinkled. I didn't know anything about wedding dresses, or dresses in general. I rarely wore them. I felt incredibly grateful that my family was here and had my back.

"What kind of beer you want?"

As I came out of the store with a six pack of Michelob, I heard Steve call me. He was annoyed because he didn't know where we had gone. That old uneasy feeling of being in trouble with my big brother surfaced. I instantly felt I had done something wrong. Ray looked puzzled, too. I had totally forgotten about him. We'd been gone three hours, and between the drinks and my wrinkled dress, I was off my game.

"Allison and Cherie are at my apartment ironing my wedding dress."

"What's with the beer?"

"It's really hot in my apartment and Allison wanted beer."

"Great."

Steve rolled his eyes and looked at Ray. His face softened, and he seemed to understand that the wrinkled dress had freaked me out. I loved my big brother.

"Just do what you gotta do, Tracy. We'll meet you back at the church before rehearsal."

I hoofed the beer to my car and relished the idea of drinking them with the two beautiful women taking care of me and my wedding dress. This was like a bachelorette party, and a couple beers would do us all good. I was about to be married!

52

Down the Aisle

Ray's dad wanted to foot the bill for the rehearsal dinner, so we decided to save his money and pack everyone into a small banquet room at Round Table Pizza. As the evening wore on, I felt a full-blown migraine brewing, which was rare. I was exhausted from all that liquor along with a pile of nerves from the rehearsal and all the attention I was getting. I was afraid I might throw up in the restaurant in front of our guests. Ray rubbed my shoulders to soothe my discomfort. That's when I heard Dad's remark to Steve Fish.

"Now there's a guy with his hands full."

I saw Steve smile and nod. I was annoyed. I didn't like being the brunt of Dad's joke, but sitting there sick as a dog, I knew he was right. Ray *did* have his hands full, now more than ever.

In the morning, our faithful wedding helpers gathered at the church to make last-minute preparations. Feeling one hundred percent better, I brought my freshly ironed wedding dress and all the makeup and hair formulas I would need to get as beautiful as possible. My two bridesmaids, Layne Fish and Sharon Buckley, were there to help me out.

In the makeshift parlor room, Allison curled my hair and put on my makeup. I still wasn't big on using it, but I have to say I looked extraordinary that day. Once I got into my dress, Allison pulled out a sachet with some knick-knacks inside. The bracelet and earrings, along with a necklace and a brooch, were something old and new, and borrowed and blue. I was clueless about the old English rhyme, but Allison assured me they were traditional good-luck objects to give the bride on her wedding day.

As she fastened the necklace I had borrowed, Gretchen came into the room.

"You look so beautiful, Tracy."

She gave me a peck on the cheek.

"Just lovely."

Dad was wearing a black shirt, black slacks, a white tie, and the same tweed jacket he always wore on special occasions. Allison picked up on it right away.

"Isn't that the jacket you wore to my wedding?"

She said it like she was trying to be funny, but it sounded like a criticism.

"That's right. It's my special coat."

He pulled it down and brushed the breast.

When Gretchen and Dad walked out, Allison was practically seething.

"I can't believe she's wearing white. Only the bride is supposed to wear white."

To me, Gretchen did nothing wrong. Her off-white dress had more lace than mine, but that didn't matter. As long as she didn't dress like a clown or a prostitute, I didn't care. It was quite pretty, and she looked cute for an older lady.

I think Allison still had it in for Gretchen. Ever since Dad's wedding, even though she didn't live far, Allison hardly spent time with them. She couldn't let go of how Gretchen had treated us when she first married Dad, from the dirty dishes in Steve's bed to kicking me out of the house. Dad hardly ever saw his new grandchild. I felt sad that our family was broken in so many ways.

Shortly before it was time for Dad to walk me down the aisle, he and Gretchen came back to wait with me. I could tell Dad was a little nervous. He didn't quite know what to say to me with all the marriage stuff going on. I don't think he knew what to do with me all dolled up the way I was. I probably looked the prettiest he'd ever seen. I could tell he wanted things to go well.

"You sure look great kiddo. With that wholesome Steingold nose and everything."

My stomach instantly rose into my throat. *How can he point out my big nose at a time like this?* My eyes flooded with tears. I turned away from Dad. He had no idea what he'd done. I couldn't tell him. It fell to Gretchen.

"Ernie! Just shut it."

"What? What did I say?"

"Get over there."

She led him out of the room and down the hall. I needed a touch up right away. I knew I looked beautiful, and my nose was not about to change the way I felt. But Dad was supposed to say something about how beautiful I was. Instead, he threw me some stupid wisecrack. Ever since I was a kid, he made fun of all our noses, his included. I was aware my nose was bigger than average, and it haunted me every day. Up until then, I had blocked my big Jewish nose out of my mind.

Allison came back in and could see the anguish all over my face.

"What's wrong?"

"Good ole Dad and his big nose jokes."

The last thing I wanted to be was a bride crying on her wedding day.

"You've got to be kidding me."

Allison was pissed.

"Dad's an idiot."

She touched the edge of my open veil.

"Let me tell you, sister. Today you have the prettiest nose on Earth. Don't you ever forget it."

I heard later that Gretchen scolded dad, and he couldn't believe I was upset.

"Why would that bother her? Must be some wedding jitters."

"No, Ernie, it's what you said. Get back in there and tell your daughter you're sorry and that she's beautiful."

I liked Gretchen a little more after I heard that. She had some great qualities, but I never got the chance to follow up.

I fixed my makeup before Dad came back. He gave me a silent hug and a kiss just before the wedding march began. He didn't say anything. He probably thought it was safer that way. I warned him to be careful not to step on my dress. He looked down at his feet, as if to make sure he didn't, and I could see he didn't want to screw up again.

As we moved down the aisle, I wished that time could stand still so I could savor these last moments with my dad. When we finally reached Ray at the altar, I was overjoyed at the sight of this handsome, kind man who loved me. I felt like the luckiest person in the world. Dad handed me off to Ray, and tiptoed around the modest train of my dress like it was a minefield. The sight of him doing that made me smile even more.

During the ceremony, Ray played me the Bread love song "If" on his trumpet, and we drank Squirt soda for communion because no one had a corkscrew to open the wine. The church was filled with people who loved us, and to top it off we had six-foot-long Subway sandwiches and potato salad for the reception.

As Ray and I were about to drive to the beach, my family came out to see us off. I didn't want to leave. It had been such a great day, surrounded by the people I loved, that I was torn between my new husband and my family. *How can I leave while they're all still there?*

I hugged and kissed everyone goodbye. They were staying another night and Dad was taking everyone to a country bar he and Gretchen had discovered. I wanted to go with them and not miss anything, but I had a date with my dreamy new husband.

Ray finally got me into the car. Dad had his arm around Gretchen as he watched us pull out of the parking lot. I'd never felt so happy and sad at the same time. I waved to all of them as we took off down the street.

As we drove, I pictured myself as a kid and Dad driving me in his van to wherever I wanted to go. Those days were gone, and the thought added to my melancholy. At the stop light, I had a happy thought. I would never again feel the need to have Dad drop me around the corner.

53
My Last Day at the Pool

Seven years later, when Ray got a job offer in Los Angeles, I knew we had to go. I loved the idea of living near Dad again. Our daughters, Emily and Julia, were two and four years old, and I was overjoyed that they would get to know their grandpa.

We rented a house a couple miles away from Dad's place. The best part was watching our daughters play with Dad in the same pool I had frolicked in as a kid. He was great with them, pushing them around in the inflatable boat. Watching him love my kids made me feel loved all over again.

Dad struggled with a bad heart, though, which had gotten progressively worse. Soon, he had to stop working and couldn't walk far without losing his breath. He was only sixty-nine and dying. I was scared, and through our many conversations, I knew he was, too.

Three days before Thanksgiving, I headed over on my weekly visit. I went straight to the pool because that's where he was likely to be. When I saw water spilling over the edge and flowing across the deck, my heart filled with dread. Dad was flat on his back next to a lounge chair. I rushed to him and put my hands on his bare chest. He was lying in the sun, so his skin felt warm. I considered CPR, but I knew right away he had been gone a while. I was helpless.

Dad died on a Monday afternoon, sunbathing at his favorite place on Earth.

Later, I left the house for the first time in my life without having my dad. I knew it would take a long time to get used to losing the one person who loved me like no one else. Eventually, I could smile at the idea of it all. Dad died exactly where it all started. I think he would be happy to know he went like that, right there at home on a sunny Southern California day.

I had come to accept any issues I had with my dad, like the many times he embarrassed me, and I was proud of him. He may not have always kept me out of trouble, but I always knew he loved me.

Three months later, we headed north. It was easy to leave Burbank with Dad no longer there. What a gift to share the last years of his life.

I have come so far since crawling around that pool and sinking to the bottom as a child and teen. How fortunate I am now to have a loving husband and two beautiful daughters. I don't always think I deserve it, but I always know how lucky I am.

ACKNOWLEDGMENTS

I'd like to thank my sister, Allison, and my brother, Steve, for their love and resolve through our childhood, and for always being positive about me writing this book.

I'm also grateful to my aunts, Barbara and Jacquie, and my uncles, Earl and Bruce, for answering my constant questions; to my cousins Darlene, Debbie, Dean, and Stuart, who had their two cents to offer; to my childhood friends who gave me their time to talk and reminisce and were resources for the book, especially Mark Hillis, Sandy Fosnagh, Cindie Neeley, Kelly Walker, Lucy Rivero, Leora and Rein, and Paeok.

I'd also like to thank my New York City editor, David Tabatsky, who saw my big picture and brought so much to this book. To the great crew at Koehler, especially Joe Coccaro, whose mastery of words and edits improved the manuscript greatly. To my agent, Nancy Rosenfeld for all her hard work and for never giving up.

Thank you to Gretchen for always loving my dad.

Thank you to my daughter, Emily, for her unwavering support, and for reading and editing drafts and telling me it's okay to let it go. You are the best musician I know. To my daughter and confidante, Julia, who is proud of her "cool mom." I am so proud of you too.

I can never thank my husband, Ray, enough for believing in me and this book from the start. I am so grateful for his reading, editing, and helping me cut to the chase. His love and support is what made this book possible.

Printed in the USA
CPSIA information can be obtained
at www.ICGtesting.com
LVHW041518251024
794809LV00002B/18